Love to knit socks

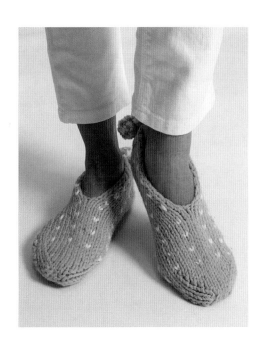

Love to knit socks

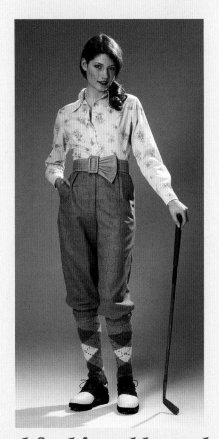

**35 fun and fashionable socks, legwarmers
and bootees to knit**

Bronwyn Lowenthal

CICO BOOKS
LONDON NEW YORK

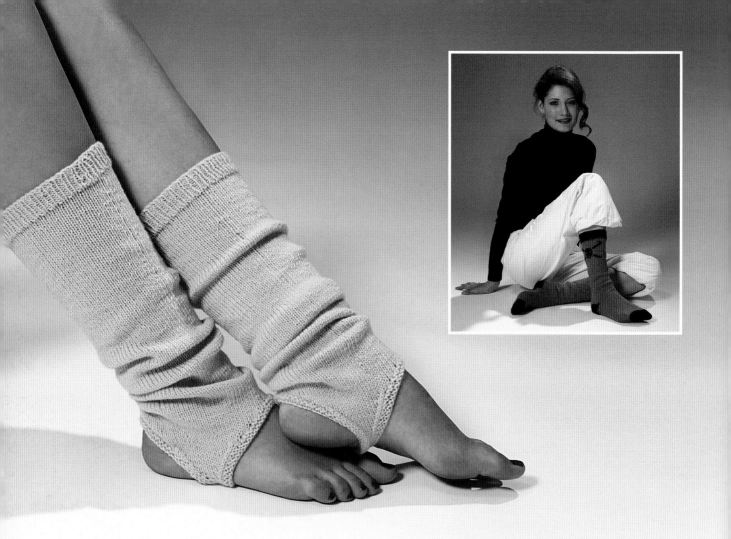

First published in 2008 by CICO Books
an imprint of Ryland Peters & Small
20–21 Jockey's Fields, London WC1R 4BW

10 9 8 7 6 5 4 3 2 1

Text © Bronwyn Lowenthal 2008
Design and photography © CICO Books 2008

Editor: Kate Haxell
Design: Liz Sephton
Design concept: Luis Peral-Aranda
Photographers: Becky Maynes and Dygo Uetsuji

A CIP catalogue record for this book is available from the
British Library

UK ISBN-13: 978 1 906094 41 6
UK ISBN-10: 1 906094 41 4

Printed in China

contents

introduction

After many years of being hidden away, subtly lurking under trousers and beneath skirts, socks and stockings are now important fashion statement pieces in their own right. From colourful, chunky designs to be worn with sneakers and jeans, to glamorous, sparkly socks that are perfect with party dresses, to sexy, lacy socks that make the most of both summer and winter wear, socks are seriously fashionable.

My love for all things knitted first started on a holiday to Turkey when I brought back some traditional Turkish socks for a few friends. My friends loved their socks so much that I was inspired to go back to Turkey the following year to find the knitters to help me start my very first Lowie knitwear collection.

In the Middle East socks and 'stockings' still hold a great place in a society where a single sock can tell a lot about the wearer: where he is from, his social rank, if he is married or single. The stockings often tell stories of love, war, natural disasters, family feuds and other memorable occasions.

Most of the socks in this book are inspired by fashion (rather than family feuds). Others are inspired by function and have been given a fresh twist to bring them up-to-date. I hope that you will find all of the designs fun to both knit and wear.

As well as socks, I have designed some other sock-related pieces. You will find legwarmers in various styles, baby bootees and a sexy stockings and suspenders set to knit.

Knitted footwear has never been so versatile. In *Love to Knit Socks* you'll find projects for flip-flop socks (far left) to add colourful flair to staple summer shoes, fun legwarmers that update an 80s classic (left) and miniature versions of comfy socks to keep little feet warm (below). Walking the dog will be a cosy outing in Fair Isle socks (top right), while soft slouchy socks are perfect for evenings in front of the TV (centre right) and practical gardening socks prove that weeding can be stylish.

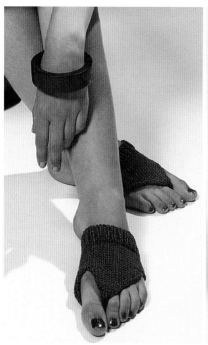

Some of the designs are popular pieces from past Lowie collections that I have often been asked for patterns for, but the vast majority of these projects have been designed specifically for *Love to Knit Socks*. My personal favourites include the gold peep-toe socks (page 12), the gardening socks with practical knee pads (page 74), the cherry slippers (page 98) and the lacy knit stockings and suspenders (pages 30–33). Whatever your tastes, you are sure to find your own favourites from the 35 projects in this book.

For those of you who need some guidance when it comes to knitting your own socks, I've included a comprehensive techniques section that will take you from the starting basics through to knitting in the round, cabling, Fair Isle and intarsia. People are sometimes put off knitting socks because they seem complicated, but many of the designs in this book are simple and the step-by-step techniques will help you complete your socks successfully. If you are an experienced knitter then you will find some imaginative and more challenging designs that will really make your fingers itch to knit.

No longer second-class undergarments, these socks are designed to be shown off and worn with pride. Vive le sock! Enjoy your new book and happy knitting.

Bronwyn Lowenthal

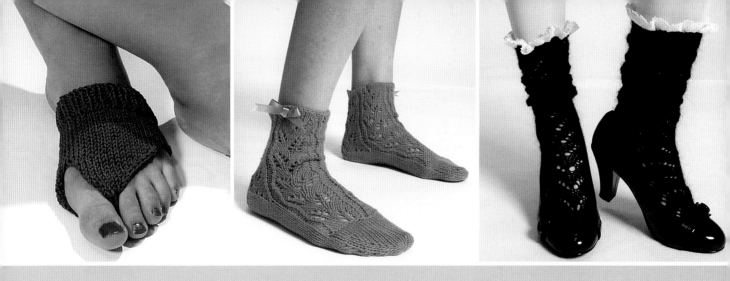

Foot fashion

These are a cute cotton option for summer and I love making them in bright colours with a contrast satin bow. They look great worn with sneakers or strappy sandals and a vintage style dress, with summer shorts or with a little playsuit.

Lacy cotton socks

pattern (both alike)

Cast on 16 sts.

Distribute these sts evenly over 3 of the double-pointed needles and, using 4th needle, work in rounds as folls:

Round 1: Knit.

Place markers on needles at beg of round and after first/last 8 sts.

Round 2: [K1, M1, k to within 1 st of marker, M1, k1] twice. *20 sts*

Round 3: Knit.

Rounds 4–15: Rep rounds 2–3 six more times. *44 sts*

Rounds 16–19: Knit, inc 1 st at end of last round. *45 sts*

Round 20: P1, k20, p24.

Now work sts on top of foot in lace patt as folls:

Round 1: P1, k20, [p1, skpo, k1, yo, k1, yo, k5, k2tog] twice.

Round 2: P1, k20, [p1, k11] twice.

Rounds 3–6: Rep rounds 1–2 twice.

Round 7: P1, k20, [p1, skpo, k6, yo, k1, yo, k2tog] twice.

Round 8: P1, k20, [p1, k11] twice.

Rounds 9–12: Rep rounds 7–8 twice.

These 12 rounds form lace patt.

Work in patt as set for a further 16 rounds, ending after patt round 4.

Shape heel

Next row: P1, k4, inc in next st, k5, [inc in next st, k4] twice, turn.

Next row: P23, turn.

Slip rem 25 sts onto a holder and now, working backwards and forwards in rows, not rounds, work on this set of 23 sts only for heel as folls:

Work in st st for 12 rows, ending after a WS row.

Next row: K14, sl 1, k2tog, psso, turn.

Next row: P6, p3tog, turn.

Next row: K6, sl 1, k2tog, psso, turn.

Rep last 2 rows twice more, then the first of these 2 rows again.

Break yarn and leave these 7 sts on a holder.

Shape leg

With RS facing and starting at base of heel sts, pick up and knit 8 sts along first row-end edge of heel, k 7 heel sts, then pick up and knit 8 sts along other row-end edge of heel, patt rem 25 sts. *48 sts*

Next round: [K11, p1] four times.

Now work in patt over all sts as folls:

Round 1: [Skpo, k6, yo, k1, yo, k2tog, p1] four times.

Round 2: [K11, p1] four times.

Rounds 3–6: Rep rounds 1–2 twice.

Round 7: [Skpo, k1, yo, k1, yo, k5, k2tog, p1] four times.

Round 8: [K11, p1] four times.

Rounds 9–12: Rep rounds 7–8 twice.

These 12 rounds form lace patt.

Cont in patt for a further 28 rounds.

Cast off loosely.

TO MAKE UP

Weave in loose ends neatly, then press carefully. Run gathering thread around cast-on edge, pull up tight and fasten off securely.

Edging

With RS facing and using 3.25mm crochet hook, attach yarn to cast off edge at back of sock, 1 ch (does NOT count as st), then work 1 dc into each cast off st around top of sock, ending with ss to first dc.

Fasten off.

Cut ribbon into 2 equal lengths and tie each piece into a bow. Attach a bow to top of each sock as in photograph.

Size
Approx 21cm from toe to heel

Yarn
One 50g ball of Rowan Cotton Glacé in orange

Needles
Set of 4 double-pointed 3.75mm knitting needles
3.25mm crochet hook

Other materials
Stitch holder
Knitter's sewing needle
50cm of beige ribbon

Tension
30 rows and 23 stitches to 10cm square over st st using 3.75mm knitting needles

Abbreviations
See page 109
ch = chain
dc = double crochet
ss = slip stitch

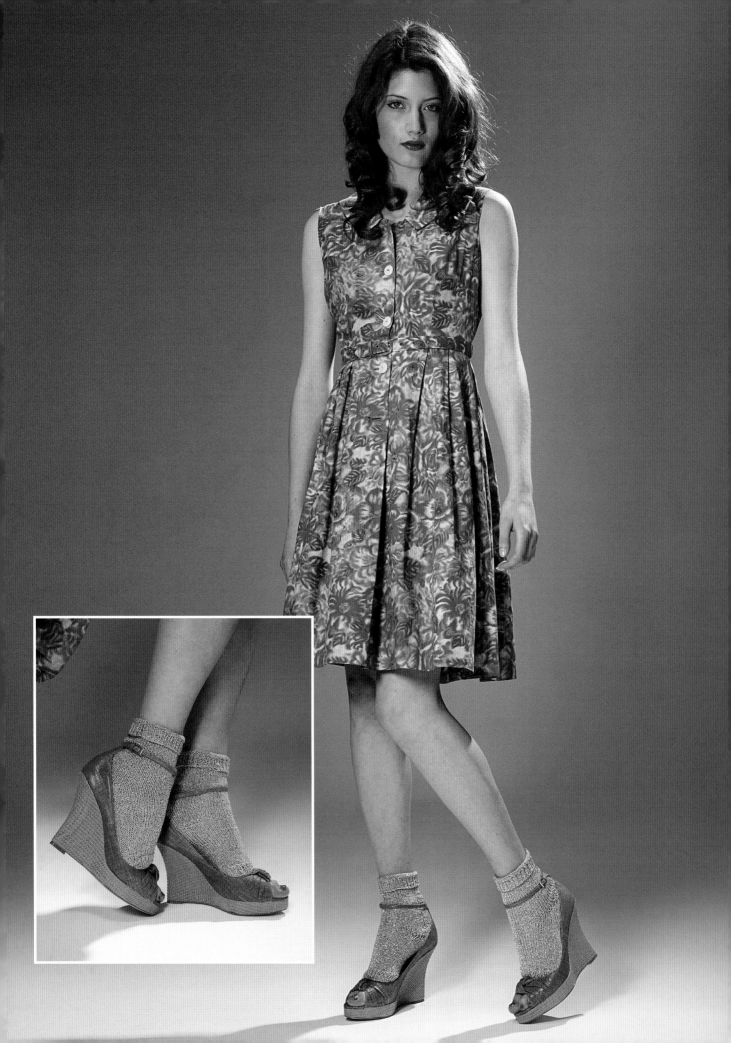

Gold peep-toe socks

pattern (both alike)

Cast on 52 sts.

Distribute these sts evenly over 3 of the double-pointed needles and, using 4th needle, work in rounds as folls:

Round 1: *K1, p1, rep from * to end.

Rep round 1 nine more times.

Round 11: Knit.

Rep round 11 until sock measures 12cm, working k2tog at end of last round. *51 sts*

Cut yarn.

Shape heel

Slip next 13 sts on 1st needle, next 13 sts on 2nd needle, next 13 sts on 3rd needle and last 12 sts on end of 1st needle.

Rejoin yarn to beg of first needle.

Now working backwards and forwards in rows, not rounds, shape heel as folls:

Next row: K24, turn.

Next row: Sl 1, p23, turn.

Next row: Sl 1, k22, turn.

Next row: Sl 1, p21, turn.

Cont in this way, working one less st on every row until the foll row has been worked:

Next row: Sl 1, p11, turn.

Next row: Sl 1, k11, turn.

Next row: Sl 1, p12, turn.

Cont in this way, working one more st on every row until the foll row has been worked:

Next row: Sl 1, p24, turn.

Slip next 17 sts on 1st needle, next 17 sts on 2nd needle and next 17 sts on 3rd needle. *51 sts*

Next round: Knit

Rep this last round until sock measures 14cm from last dec row, decreasing one st at end of last round. *50 sts*

Next round: *K1, p1, rep from * to end.

Rep this last round nine more times.

Cast off in rib.

TO MAKE UP

Weave in loose ends neatly.

What fun! These socks look amazing with open-toed high heels, especially as an evening option. Add brightly coloured nail polish for some extra wow factor. Peep-toe socks also look great with flip-flops and mules.

Size
To fit shoe size 4–6

Yarn
Two 25g balls of Arista Crochet yarn in gold

Needles
Set of 4 double-pointed 2.75mm knitting needles

Other materials
Knitter's sewing needle

Tension
42 rows and 30 stitches to 10cm square over st st using 2.75mm needles

Abbreviations
See page 109

My little flip-flop socks will stop your shoes from rubbing against your skin, as well as looking good. A contrast colour is heaps of fun, but if you choose to make the socks the same colour as your shoes they will look like a quirky extension of your footwear.

Flip-flop socks

pattern (both alike)

Cast on 48 sts.

Distribute these sts evenly over 3 of the double-pointed needles and, using 4th needle, work in rounds as folls:

Rounds 1–6: *K1, p1, rep from * to end.

Rounds 7–15: Knit.

Round 16: Knit to last 6 sts, cast off 6 sts.

Round 17: Cast off 6 sts, knit to end. *36 sts*

Working backwards and forwards in rows, not rounds, cont in st st, starting with a purl row, as folls:

Next row: P2tog, purl to last 2 sts, p2togtbl. *34 sts*

Next row: K2togtbl, k13, k2tog, turn, leaving rem 17 sts on a holder.

Work on these 15 sts only for first section.

Next row: P2tog, purl to last 2 sts, p2togtbl.

Next row: K2togtbl, knit to last 2 sts, k2tog.

Next row: Purl to last 2 sts, p2togtbl.

Next row: K2togtbl, knit to last 2 sts, k2tog.

Next row: Purl to last 2 sts, p2togtbl.

Next row: K2togtbl, knit to end.

Next row: Purl.

Next row: K2togtbl, knit to last 2 sts, k2tog.

Next row: Purl.

Next row: K2togtbl, knit to end. *3 sts*

Work 1 row, ending after a WS row.

Break yarn, leaving sts on needle.

Rejoin yarn to other set of 17 sts and rejoin yarn with RS facing.

Next row: K2togtbl, k13, k2tog.

Next row: P2tog, purl to last 2 sts, p2togtbl.

Next row: K2togtbl, knit to last 2 sts, k2tog.

Next row: P2togtbl, purl to end.

Next row: K2togtbl, knit to last 2 sts, k2tog.

Next row: P2togtbl, purl to end.

Next row: Knit to last 2 sts, k2tog.

Next row: Purl.

Next row: K2togtbl, knit to last 2 sts, k2tog.

Next row: Purl.

Next row: Knit to last 2 sts, k2tog. *3 sts*

Work 1 row, ending after a WS row.

Break yarn, leaving a fairly long end and sts on needle.

Slip first set of 3 sts onto one needle, and other set of 3 sts onto another needle.

Using long end left at end of second section, graft together sts from both needles.

TO MAKE UP

Weave in loose ends neatly, then press carefully.

Size
Approx 21cm around foot

Yarn
One 50g ball of Rowan Cotton Glacé in purple

Needles
Set of 4 double-pointed 3.25mm knitting needles

Other materials
Stitch holder
Knitter's sewing needle

Tension
32 rows and 23 stitches to 10cm square over st st using 3.25mm needles

Abbreviations
See page 109

> **"Knitting these in a contrast colour is heaps of fun."**

Flower socks

pattern (both alike)

Using A, cast on 18 sts.

Distribute these sts evenly over 3 of the double-pointed needles and, using 4th needle, work in rounds as folls:

Round 1: Knit.

Place markers on needles at beg of round and after first/last 9 sts.

Round 2: [M1, K to marker, slip marker onto right needle] twice.

Round 3: [K to marker, M1, slip marker onto right needle] twice. *22 sts*

Rounds 4–9: Rep rounds 2–3 three more times. *34 sts*

Keeping increases as now set (by inc 2 sts on every round and alternating which side of markers these incs are worked), now work in patt from chart as folls:

Joining in and breaking off colours as required and stranding yarn not in use loosely across WS of work, work rounds 1–10. *54 sts* (All toe increases completed.)

Work 4 rounds, inc 1 st at end of last round. *55 sts*

Work 9 rounds, dec 1 st at end of last round. *54 sts*

Work 6 rounds. (Chart round 29 completed.)

Noting that central 11 sts on top of foot are worked in an 18-round patt rep and rem sts are worked in a 13-round patt rep, now cont in patt following chart as folls:

Work 21 rounds.

Shape heel

Next round: K27, turn and using A cast on 27 sts.

Slip rem 27 sts of foot section onto a holder and distribute these 54 sts evenly over 3 of the double-pointed needles.

Using 4th needle and A only, work in rounds as folls:

Next round: Knit.

Rep last round four more times.

Next round: [K1, skpo, k21, k2tog, k1] twice. *50 sts*

Next round: [K1, skpo, k19, k2tog, k1] twice. *46 sts*

Next round: [K1, skpo, k17, k2tog, k1] twice. *42 sts*

Next round: [K1, skpo, k15, k2tog, k1] twice. *38 sts*

Next round: [K1, skpo, k13, k2tog, k1] twice. *34 sts*

Next round: [K1, skpo, k11, k2tog, k1] twice. *30 sts*

Next round: [K1, skpo, k9, k2tog, k1] twice. *26 sts*

Just as easily worn for dressing up as for dressing down, these flower socks are very versatile and girlie. I love the traditional flower pattern, which in magenta with green leaves on the cream background gives the socks a Victoriana feel.

Size
Approx 21cm from toe to heel

Yarn
Two 50g balls of Rowan Pure Wool DK in cream (A) and one ball in each of magenta (B) and green (C)

Needles
Set of 4 double-pointed 3.25mm knitting needles

Other materials
Stitch holder
Knitter's sewing needle

Tension
36 rows and 25 stitches to 10cm square over patt using 3.25mm needles

Abbreviations
See page 109

FLOWER SOCKS

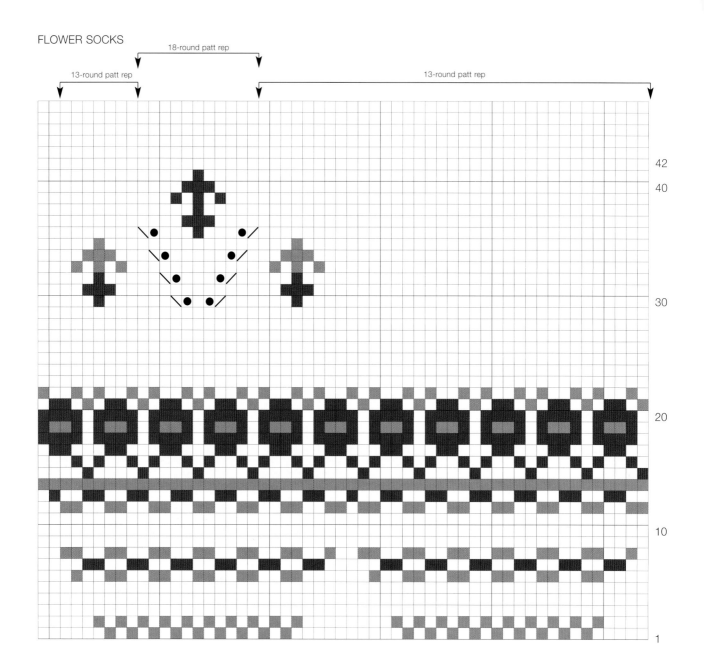

KEY

- ☐ cream
- ▨ green
- ▪ magenta
- ╱ k2tog
- ╲ skpo
- ● yo

Next round: [K1, skpo, k7, k2tog, k1] twice. *22 sts*

Next round: [K1, skpo, k5, k2tog, k1] twice. *18 sts*

Next round: [K1, skpo, k3, k2tog, k1] twice. *14 sts*

Next round: [K1, skpo, k1, k2tog, k1] twice. *10 sts*

Next round: [K1, sl 1, k2tog, psso, k1] twice. *6 sts*

Break yarn and thread through rem 6 sts. Pull up tight and fasten off securely.

Shape leg

Return to sts of foot section and, with RS facing and using A, pick up and knit 27 sts from cast-on edge of heel, patt rem 27 sts of foot section. *54 sts*

Distribute these sts evenly over 3 of the double-pointed needles and, using 4th needle, work in rounds as folls:

Keeping patt on top of foot (now front of leg) correct as set, cont following chart until all 18 rounds of central 11 st patt rep have been worked five times in total.

Next round: *K2, p1, rep from * to end. Rep last round twenty-three more times. Cast off in rib.

TO MAKE UP

Weave in ends neatly, then press carefully. Join toe seam.

"These flower socks are very versatile and girlie."

These Japanese-inspired socks with separate big toes were originally worn with wooden sandals by geishas and with cotton split-toe shoes by martial artists. Modern girls can wear them with sandals or flip-flops for an interesting summer option.

Size
Approx 23cm from toe to heel

Yarn
Two 50g balls of Rowan Cotton Glacé in red

Needles
Set of 4 double-pointed 3.25mm knitting needles

Other materials
Stitch holder
Knitter's sewing needle

Tension
32 rows and 23 stitches to 10cm square over st st using 3.25mm needles

Abbreviations
See page 109

Tabi socks

pattern

Cast on 42 sts.
Distribute these sts evenly over 3 of the double-pointed needles and, using 4th needle, work in rounds as folls:
Rounds 1–5: *K1, p1, rep from * to end.
Rounds 6–15: Knit.
Shape heel
Left sock only
Row 1: K20, wrap next st, turn.
Right sock only
Row 1: K41, wrap next st, turn.
Both socks
Now working backwards and forwards in rows, not rounds, shape heel as folls:
Row 2: P18, wrap next st, turn.
Row 3: K17, wrap next st, turn.
Row 4: P16, wrap next st, turn.
Row 5: K15, wrap next st, turn.
Row 6: P14, wrap next st, turn.
Row 7: K13, wrap next st, turn.
Row 8: P12, wrap next st, turn.
Row 9: K11, wrap next st, turn.
Row 10: P10, wrap next st, turn.
Row 11: K11, turn.
Row 12: P12, turn.
Row 13: K13, turn.
Row 14: P14, turn.
Row 15: K15, turn.
Row 16: P16, turn.
Row 17: K17, turn.
Row 18: P18, turn.
Row 19: K19, turn.
Row 20: P20, turn.
Row 21: Knit to end of round, re-distributing all 42 sts over 3 of the 4 needles.
Next round: Knit.
Rep last round until sock measures 15cm from last heel row.

Shape main toe section
Next round: K14, slip next 14 sts onto a holder (for big toe section), turn and cast on 2 sts, turn and k rem 14 sts of round.
Re-distribute these 30 sts over 3 of the 4 needles and cont as folls:
Work 4 rounds.
Next round: [K2tog, k11, sl 1, k1, psso] twice. *26 sts*
Work 2 rounds.
Next round: [K2tog, k9, sl 1, k1, psso] twice. *22 sts*
Work 2 rounds.
Next round: [K2tog, k7, sl 1, k1, psso] twice. *18 sts*
Work 2 rounds.
Slip first 9 sts onto one needle and last 9 sts onto another needle. Join toe seam by grafting sts from both needles together.

Shape big toe section
Rejoin yarn at base of main toe section, pick up and knit 1 st from cast-on sts at base of main toe section, k 14 sts left on holder, then pick up and knit a second st from base of main toe section.
Re-distribute these 16 sts over 3 of the 4 needles and cont as folls:
Work 7 rounds.
Next round: [K2tog, k4, sl 1, k1, psso] twice. *12 sts*
Work 5 rounds.
Slip first 6 sts onto one needle and last 6 sts onto another needle. Join toe seam by grafting sts from both needles together.

TO MAKE UP
Weave in ends neatly, then press carefully.

"Use a delicate lace in an off-white colour for a vintage feel."

Lacy long socks

I just love these lacy knit socks with lace trim. Use a delicate lace in an off-white colour for a vintage feel. I find that cotton lace looks best and it's much nicer to touch than nylon. These socks will also look cute peeking out of ankle or calf-length boots.

pattern (both alike)

Cast on 18 sts.

Distribute these sts evenly over 3 of the double-pointed needles and, using 4th needle, work in rounds as folls:

Round 1: Knit.

Place markers on needles at beg of round and after first/last 9 sts.

Round 2: [K1, M1, k to within 1 st of marker, M1, k1] twice. *22 sts*

Round 3: Knit.

Rounds 4–15: Rep rounds 2–3 six more times. *46 sts*

Rounds 16–20: Knit, removing markers after first/last 9 sts on first round.

Work top of foot in lace patt as folls:

Round 21: K25, [yo, k3, sl 1, k2tog, psso, k3, yo, k1] twice, k1.

Round 22: Knit.

Round 23: K25, [k1, yo, k2, sl 1, k2tog, psso, k2, yo, k2] twice, k1.

Round 24: Knit.

Round 25: K25, [k2, yo, k1, sl 1, k2tog, psso, k1, yo, k3] twice, k1.

Round 26: Knit.

Round 27: K25, [k3, yo, sl 1, k2tog, psso, yo, k4] twice, k1.

Round 28: Knit.

Rounds 21–28 form patt.

Work in patt for a further 16 rounds.

Shape heel

Next round: K23, turn.

Slip rem 23 sts onto a holder and now, working backwards and forwards in rows, not rounds, work on this set of 23 sts only for heel as folls:

Work in st st for 11 rows, ending after a WS row.

Next row: K15, k2tog, turn.

Next row: P8, p2tog, turn.

Next row: K8, k2tog, turn.

Rep last 2 rows five more times, then the first of these 2 rows again.

Break yarn and leave these 9 sts on a holder.

Shape leg

With RS facing and starting at base of heel sts (end of last complete round), pick up and knit 7 sts along first row-end edge of heel, k 9 heel sts, then pick up and knit 7 sts along other row-end edge of heel, patt rem 23 sts. *46 sts*

Next round: K5, k2tog, k4, k2tog, k3, skpo, k5, patt to end. *43 sts*

Keeping patt correct as set over sts on top of foot, now work in patt over sts at back of leg as folls:

Round 1: *K1, yo, k2, sl 1, k2tog, psso, k2, yo, k2, rep from * once more, patt to end.

Round 2: Knit.

Round 3: *K2, yo, k1, sl 1, k2tog, psso, k1, yo, k3, rep from * once more, patt to end.

Round 4: Knit.

Round 5: *K3, yo, sl 1, k2tog, psso, yo, k4, rep from * once more, patt to end.

Round 6: Knit.

Round 7: *Yo, k3, sl 1, k2tog, psso, k3, yo, k1, rep from * once more, patt to end.

Round 8: Knit.

These 8 rounds form patt.

Cont in patt for a further 54 rounds, dec 1 st at end of last round. *42 sts*

Next round: *K1, p1, rep from * to end.

Rep last round six more times.

Cast off loosely.

TO MAKE UP

Weave in ends neatly, then press carefully. Join toe seam.

Cut lace into 2 equal lengths and join ends to form 2 loops. Run gathering thread around straight edge and pull up to fit cast off edge of sock. Slip stitch lace in place, ensuring edge will still stretch to fit leg.

Size
Approx 21cm from toe to heel

Yarn
Two 25g balls of Rowan Kidsilk Haze (used double) in black

Needles
Set of 4 double-pointed 4mm knitting needles

Other materials
Stitch holder
Knitter's sewing needle
80cm of cream cotton lace

Tension
30 rows and 22 stitches to 10cm square over st st using 4mm needles

Abbreviations
See page 109

These classic British chunky cabled socks are knitted in a tweedy Shetland yarn for authenticity. Even though I couldn't resist dressing them up with a natural coloured knit dress and tan leather heels, they are essentially weekend casual socks and will look great with jeans and boots.

Cabled socks

pattern (both alike)

Cast on 38 sts.

Distribute these sts evenly over 3 of the double-pointed needles and, using 4th needle, work in rounds as folls:

Round 1: [K2, p1] twice, [inc once in each of next 2 sts, p1, k2, p1] five times, k2. *48 sts*

Now work in cable and rib patt as folls:

Round 2: [K2, p1] twice, [k4, p1, k2, p1] five times, k2.

Round 3: [K2, p1] twice, [C4B, p1, k2, p1] five times, k2.

Rounds 4–6: As round 2.

Rounds 2–6 form cable and rib patt.

Cont in patt for a further 2 rounds.

Round 9: M1, patt to end. *49 sts*

Round 10: P1, patt to end, M1. *50 sts*

Round 11: P1, patt to last st, p1.

Cont as set for a further 43 rounds.

Round 55: P1, skpo, patt to last 3 sts, k2tog, p1. *48 sts*

Work 9 rounds.

Work last 10 rounds twice more. *44 sts*

Break off yarn.

Shape heel

Slip first 11 sts and last 11 sts of last round onto one needle (for heel), and rem 22 sts onto holders (for top of foot).

With RS facing, join yarn to 22 heel sts. Working backwards and forwards in rows, not rounds, work on these 22 sts only for heel as folls:

Row 1: K3, [k2tog] twice, k8, [k2tog] twice, k3. *18 sts*

Starting with a purl row, work in st st on these 18 sts for 7 rows, ending after a WS row.

Next row: K12, skpo, turn.

Next row: P7, p2tog, turn.

Next row: K7, skpo, turn.

Rep last 2 rows three more times, then first of these rows again. *8 sts*

Break yarn.

Next row: K4 but do NOT turn. (Heel completed.)

Working in rounds again, distributing all sts evenly over 3 needles, start to shape foot as folls:

Next round: Knit rem 4 sts of heel, pick up and knit 5 sts down row-end edge of heel, patt next 22 sts, pick up and knit 5 sts up other row-end edge of heel, knit first 4 heel sts. *40 sts*

Next round: [P1, k2] three times, patt 22 sts, [k2, p1] three times.

This round sets the sts – sts on top of foot still in cable patt with sole sts now in rib.

Cont as set for a further 24 rounds.

Shape toe

Round 1: K11, k2tog, k5, [k2tog] twice, k5, k2tog, k11. *36 sts*

Round 2: [K7, k2tog, skpo, k7] twice. *32 sts*

Round 3: Knit.

Round 4: [K6, k2tog, skpo, k6] twice. *28 sts*

Round 5: Knit.

Round 6: [K5, k2tog, skpo, k5] twice. *24 sts*

Round 7: Knit.

Round 8: [K4, k2tog, skpo, k4] twice. *20 sts*

Round 9: Knit.

Break yarn.

Slip first and last 5 sts onto one needle, and rem 10 sts onto another needle.

Graft together sts from both needles to close toe.

TO MAKE UP

Weave in ends neatly.

Size
Approx 21cm from toe to heel

Yarn
Three 50g balls of Jamieson's Soft Shetland in green

Needles
Set of 4 double-pointed 4mm knitting needles

Other materials
Cable needle
Stitch holder
Knitter's sewing needle

Tension
20 rows and 16 stitches to 10cm square over st st using 4mm needles

Abbreviations
See page 109
C4B = slip next 2 sts onto cable needle and leave at back of work, k2, then k2 from cable needle

"These socks will also look great with jeans and boots."

Turkish socks

pattern (both alike)

Using A, cast on 40 sts loosely. Distribute these sts evenly over 3 of the double-pointed needles and, using 4th needle, work in rounds as folls:

Rounds 1–21: *K3, p1tbl, rep from * to end.

Round 22: *K1, inc in next st, k1, p1tbl, rep from * to end. *50 sts*

Joining in and breaking off yarns as required and stranding yarn not in use loosely across WS of work, now work in patt from chart as folls:

Work all 18 rounds.

Using F instead of C and G instead of D, work all 18 rounds again.

Using H instead of C and J instead of D, work all 18 rounds again.

Shape heel

Next round: Using B k25, turn and using L cast on 25 sts.

Break off B.

Slip rem 25 sts of main section onto a holder and distribute these 50 sts evenly over 3 of the double-pointed needles. Using 4th needle and L, work in rounds as folls:

Next round: Using L, knit.

Rep last round twice more.

Join in M.

Next round: Using M k2, *using L k2, using M k2, rep from * to end.

Next round: Using L k1, *using M k2, using L k2, rep from * to last st, using M k1.

Next round: Using L k2, *using M k2,

These colourful socks are a traditional Turkish product and are a firm favourite of mine all through the winter. They are fabulous for curling up in front of the TV, as bed socks or worn out with Birkenstocks and jeans.

Size
Approx 23cm from toe to heel

Yarn
One 50g ball of Debbie Bliss Rialto Aran in each of olive green (A), black (B), brick red (C), pistachio green (D), white (E), dull pale green (F), tan (G), red (H), jade green (J), pale blue (L), fuchsia pink (M), dark lilac (N), lemon (Q) and peach (R)

Needles
Set of 4 double-pointed 4.5mm knitting needles

Other materials
Stitch holders
Knitter's sewing needle

Tension
26 rows and 23 stitches to 10cm square over patt using 4.5mm needles

Abbreviations
See page 109

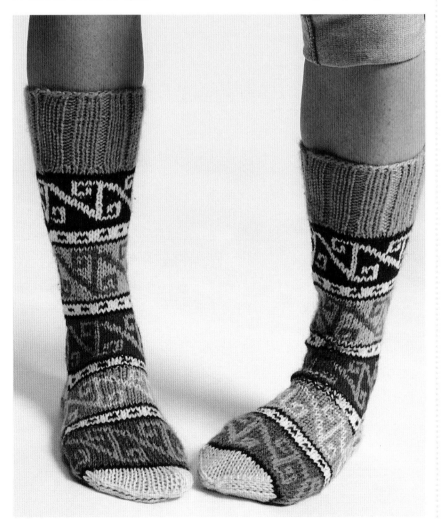

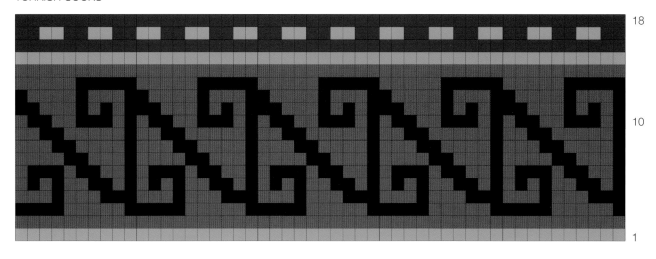

18

10

1

KEY

▨	B
▩	C
■	D
▦	E

using L k2, rep from * to end.
Break off M and complete heel using
L only.
Next round: [K1, skpo, k19, k2tog, k1]
twice. *46 sts*
**Next round: [K1, skpo, k17, k2tog,
k1] twice. *42 sts*
Next round: [K1, skpo, k15, k2tog, k1]
twice. *38 sts*
Next round: [K1, skpo, k13, k2tog, k1]
twice. *34 sts*
Next round: [K1, skpo, k11, k2tog, k1]
twice. *30 sts*
Next round: [K1, skpo, k9, k2tog, k1]
twice. *26 sts*
Next round: [K1, skpo, k7, k2tog, k1]
twice. *22 sts*
Next round: [K1, skpo, k5, k2tog, k1]
twice. *18 sts*
Next round: [K1, skpo, k3, k2tog, k1]
twice. *14 sts*
Next round: [K1, skpo, k1, k2tog, k1]
twice. *10 sts*
Next round: [K1, sl 1, k2tog, psso, k1]
twice. *6 sts*
Break yarn and thread through rem
6 sts. Pull up tight and fasten off
yarn securely.**
Shape foot
Return to sts of main section and, with
RS facing and using B, pick up and knit
25 sts from cast-on edge of heel, k rem
25 sts of main section. *50 sts*
Distribute these sts evenly over 3 of the

double-pointed needles and, using 4th
needle, work in rounds as folls:
Starting with round 2 and using N
instead of C and Q instead of D, work
rounds 2 to 18 of chart.
Using G instead of C and J instead of
D, work all 18 rounds of chart again.
Shape toe
Next round: Using B, [k1, skpo, k19,
k2tog, k1] twice. *46 sts*
Break off all contrasts, join in R.
Using R only, complete toe as for heel
from ** to **.

TO MAKE UP
Weave in ends neatly, then press
carefully.

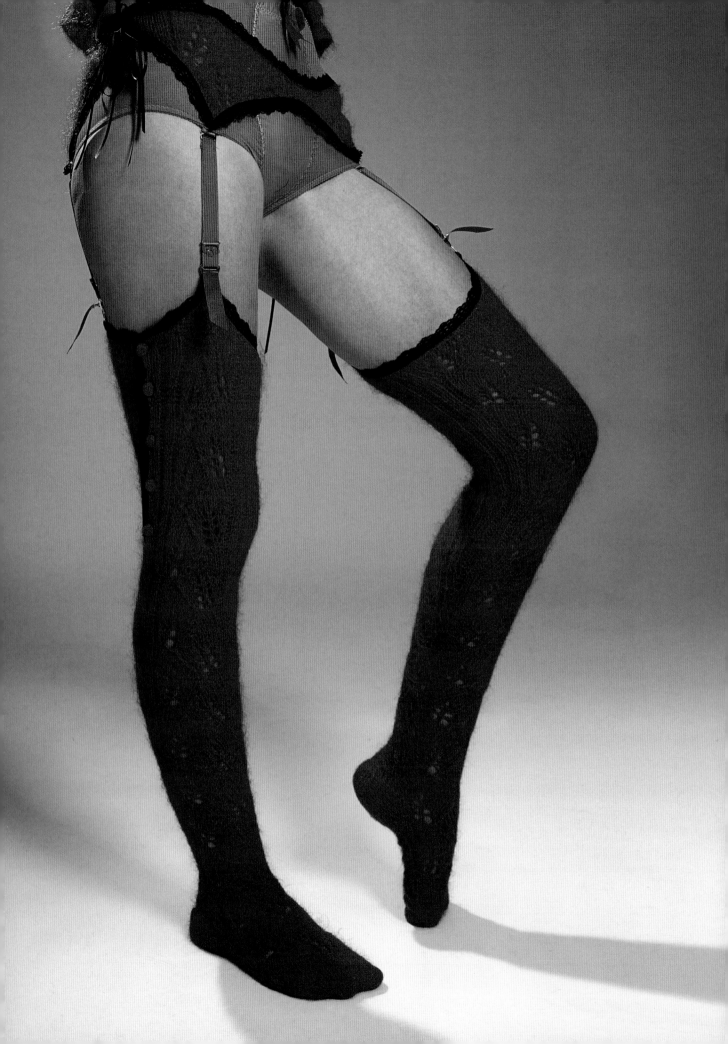

Lacy stockings and suspenders

In red and black these two sexy, fun items have a Parisian Moulin Rouge feel, but in white they will look great with a grey or black winter day dress. The lace knit may prove tricky but the results are worth the effort. Elasticated lace trim helps keep up the stockings and I've added ribbon ties to the garter belt so one size fits all.

Size
Approx 23cm from toe to heel

Yarn
Five 25g balls of Rowan Kidsilk Haze (used double) in red

Needles
Set of 4 double-pointed 4mm knitting needles

Other materials
Stitch holder
120cm of black lace
10 buttons

Tension
30 rows and 22 stitches to 10cm square over st st using 4mm needles

Abbreviations
See page 109

stockings

Cast on 16 sts.
Distribute these sts evenly over 3 of the double-pointed needles and, using 4th needle, work in rounds as folls:
Round 1: Knit.
Place markers on needles at beg of round and after first/last 8 sts.
Round 2: [K1, M1, k to within 1 st of marker, M1, k1] twice. *20 sts*
Round 3: Knit.
Rounds 4–15: As rounds 2–3 six times. *44 sts*
Remove markers.
Round 16: Knit to last st, M1, k1. *45 sts*
Round 17: Knit.
Round 18: Knit to last 3 sts.
Redistribute sts over needles so that this point becomes new point to start and end rounds.
Now work in lace patt as folls:
Round 19: [K9, k3tog, yo, k1, yo, p2] three times.
Round 20: [K13, p2] three times.
Round 21: *K7, k3tog, [k1, yo] twice, k1, p2, rep from * twice more.
Round 22: [K13, p2] three times.
Round 23: [K5, k3tog, k2, yo, k1, yo, k2, p2] three times.
Round 24: [K13, p2] three times.
Round 25: [K3, k3tog, k3, yo, k1, yo, k3, p2] three times.
Round 26: [K13, p2] three times.
Round 27: [yo, k1, yo, sl 1, k2tog, psso, k9, p2] three times.
Round 28: [K13, p2] three times.
Round 29: *K1, [yo, k1] twice, sl 1, k2tog, psso, k7, p2, rep from * twice more.
Round 30: [K13, p2] three times.
Round 31: [K2, yo, k1, yo, k2, sl 1, k2tog, psso, k5, p2] three times.
Round 32: [K13, p2] three times.

Round 33: [K3, yo, k1, yo, k3, sl 1, k2tog, psso, k3, p2] three times.
Round 34: [K13, p2] three times.
Rounds 19–34 form patt – 3 lace panels with 2 purl sts between each panel. (First and 2nd lace panels sit on top of foot, while 3rd panel sits over base of foot.)
Work in patt for a further 20 rounds, ending after round 22.
Break yarn.
Shape heel
Slip 13 sts of lace panel that runs along base of foot and the 5 sts either side of this (23 sts in total) onto one needle and slip rem 22 sts (rem 10 sts of each of the other 2 lace panels and the 2 purl sts between them) onto a holder.
Now, working backwards and forwards in rows, not rounds, work on this set of 23 sts only for heel as folls:
Rejoin yarn with RS facing and, starting with a knit row, work in st st for 14 rows, ending after a WS row.
**Next row: K14, k2tog, turn.
Next row: P6, p2tog, turn.
Next row: K6, k2tog, turn.
Rep last 2 rows six more times, then first of these 2 rows again.
Break yarn and leave these 7 sts on a holder.**
Carefully pick up and knit 23 sts from behind 23 sts of first heel section (for heel lining) and, starting with a purl row, work in st st for 13 rows, ending after a WS row.
Rep from ** to ** again.
Shape leg
With RS facing and starting at base of heel sts and picking up sts through both outer heel and heel lining, pick up and knit 8 sts up first row-end edge of heel, k7 heel sts working one st from outer heel together with one st from

heel lining, then pick up and knit 8 sts down other row-end edge of heel. Redistribute all 45 sts over 3 needles, positioning new start and end point of rounds after first 5 picked-up sts along first side of heel.

Rejoin yarn and, using 4th needle, now work in rounds again as folls:

Starting with round 23, cont straight in patt (lace panels with purl sts between) until round 26 has been worked for the 5th time (from start of patt).

Next round: [Patt 13 sts, inc once purlwise in each of next 2 sts] three times. *51 sts*

Next round: [Patt 13 sts, p4] three times.

Rep last round fourteen more times.

Next round: [Patt 13 sts, p2, M1, p2] three times. *54 sts*

Next round: [Patt 13 sts, p2, inc in next st, p2] three times. *57 sts*

Next round: [Patt 13 sts, p2, inc once knitwise in each of next 2 sts, p2] three times. *63 sts*

Next round: [Patt 13 sts, p2, k4, p2] three times.

Rep last round twelve more times.

Next round: [Patt 13 sts, p2, k1, inc once in each of next 2 sts, k1, p2] three times. *69 sts*

Next round: *Patt 13 sts, [p2, k2] twice, p2, rep from * twice more.

Rep last round six more times.

Next round: [Patt 13 sts, p2, k2, inc once purlwise in each of next 2 sts, k2, p2] three times. *75 sts*

Next round: [Patt 13 sts, p2, k2, p4, k2, p2] three times.

Rep last round six more times.

Next round: [Patt 13 sts, p2, k2, p1, inc once purlwise in each of next 2 sts, p1, k2, p2] three times. *81 sts*

Next round: *Patt 13 sts, [p2, k2] three times, p2, rep from * twice more.

Rep last round six more times.

Next round: [Patt 13 sts, p2, k2, p2, inc once purlwise in each of next 2 sts, p2, k2, p2] three times. *87 sts*

Next round: [Patt 13 sts, p2, k2, p2,

k4, p2, k2, p2] three times.

Rep last round until all 16 patt rounds of lace panels have been worked a total of nine times (from start of patt), ending after patt round 34.

Break yarn.

Left stocking only

Redistribute sts over needles so that new starting point is 6 sts after lace panel that runs up back of leg from heel.

Keeping patt correct over all sts but now working in rows, not rounds, cont as folls:

Next row: Patt to end.

Next row (WS): Cast on and purl 4 sts, patt to end. *91 sts*

Next row: K2, yo, k2tog (to make a buttonhole), patt to end.

Right stocking only

Redistribute sts over needles so that new starting point is 6 sts before lace panel that runs up back of leg from heel.

Keeping patt correct over all sts but now working in rows, not rounds, cont as folls:

Next row: Cast on and knit 4 sts, patt to end. *91 sts*

Next row (WS): Patt to end.

Next row: Patt to last 4 sts, k2tog, yo (to make a buttonhole), k2.

Both stockings

Making a further 4 buttonholes, in same way as for first buttonhole, on every foll 10th row, work a further 45 rows.

Cast off.

TO MAKE UP

Weave in ends neatly, then press carefully. Join toe seam. Sew cast-on edge of opening (near top of leg) in place on inside.

Cut lace into 2 equal lengths. Using photograph as a guide, slip stitch lace in place to top (cast off) edge and down front edge of leg opening. Sew on buttons to align with buttonholes.

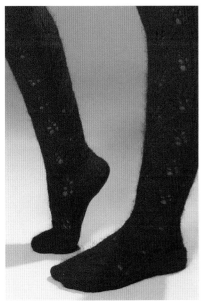

suspender belt

Front and Back (both alike)

First section

Cast on 5 sts.

Row 1: Knit.

Row 2: Inc in first st, p3, inc in last st.

Row 3: Inc in first st, k1, k3tog, yo, k1, yo, inc in last st.

Row 4: Inc purlwise in first st, k1, p6, inc purlwise in last st.

Row 5: Inc in first st, k1, k3tog, [k1, yo] twice, k1, p1, k1, inc in last st. *13 sts*

Row 6: Inc in first st, p2, k1, p8, inc in last st.

Row 7: Inc in first st, k1, k3tog, k2, yo, k1, yo, k2, p1, k3, inc in last st.

Row 8: Inc in first st, p4, k1, p10, inc in last st.

Row 9: Inc in first st, k1, k3tog, k3, yo, k1, yo, k3, p1, k5, inc in last st.

Row 10: Inc in first st, p6, k1, p12, inc in last st. *23 sts*

Row 11: Inc in first st, yo, k1, yo, sl 1, k2tog, psso, k9, p1, yo, k1, yo, sl 1, k2tog, psso, k3, inc in last st. *25 sts*

Row 12: Cast on 8 sts, work across these 8 sts as folls: p3, k1, p4, work across rem sts as folls: p9, k1, p13, k1, inc in last st. *34 sts*

Row 13: Inc in first st, k1, p1, *[k1, yo] twice, k1, sl 1, k2tog, psso, k7, p1, rep from * once more, k3.

Row 14: P3, [k1, p13] twice, k1, p2, inc in last st. *36 sts*

Break yarn and leave sts on a holder.

Second section

Work as given for first section to end of row 11. *25 sts*

Row 12: Inc in first st, p8, k1, p13, k1, inc purlwise in last st. *27 sts*

Row 13: Cast on and knit 5 sts, k2, p1, [k1, yo] twice, k1, sl 1, k2tog, psso, k7, p1, [k1, yo] twice, k1, sl 1, k2tog, psso, k3, inc in last st. *33 sts*

Row 14: Inc in first st, p10, k1, p13, k1, p7. *34 sts*

Join sections

Row 15: Work across 34 sts of second section as folls: k7, p1, k2, yo, k1, yo, k2, sl 1, k2tog, psso, k5, p1, k2, yo, k1, yo, k2, sl 1, k2tog, psso, k4, turn and cast on 9 sts, turn and work across

36 sts of first section as folls: k4, p1, [k2, yo, k1, yo, k2, sl 1, k2tog, psso, k5, p1] twice, k3. *79 sts*

Row 16: P3, [k1, p13] twice, k1, p11, [k1, p13] twice, k1, p7.

Row 17: k7, *p1, k3, yo, k1, yo, k3, sl 1, k2tog, psso, k3*, rep from * to * once more, p1, k11, rep from * to * twice more, p1, k3.

Row 18: As row 16.

Row 19: k7, *p1, k9, k3tog, yo, k1, yo*, rep from * to * once more, p1, k11, rep from * to * twice more, p1, k3.

Row 20: As row 16.

Cast off.

TO MAKE UP

Weave in ends neatly, then press carefully.

Using photograph as a guide, sew lace to entire outer edge of Front and Back. Cut ribbon into 8 equal lengths and attach 2 pieces to each side (row-end) edge of Front and Back. Tie Front and Back together at sides using ribbons. Sew attachments for stockings to back of points of suspender belt.

Size
Adjustable to fit hips 81–97cm

Yarn
One 25g ball of Rowan Kidsilk Haze (used double) in red

Needles
Pair of 4mm knitting needles

Other materials
Stitch holder
2m of black lace
2.60m of narrow black satin ribbon
Purchased suspender belt attachments for stockings

Tension
30 rows and 22 stitches to 10cm square over st st using 4mm needles

Abbreviations
See page 109

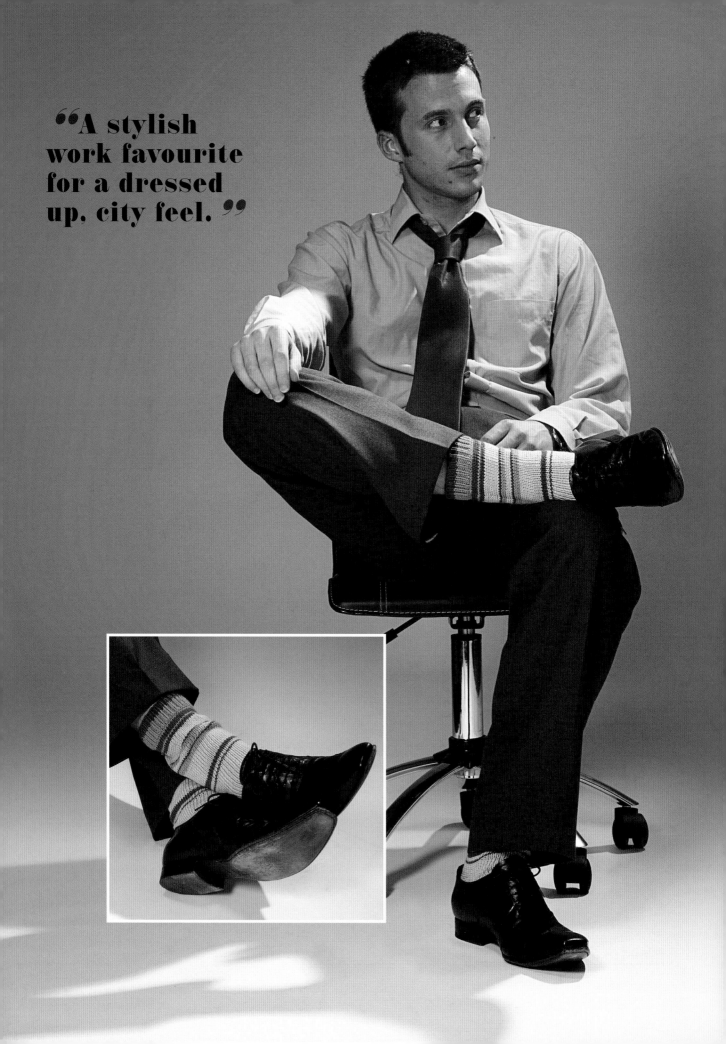

"A stylish work favourite for a dressed up, city feel."

Men's city socks

pattern (both alike)

Using A, cast on 60 sts.

Distribute these sts evenly over 3 of the double-pointed needles and, using 4th needle, work in rounds as folls:

Rounds 1–4: Using A, *k1, p1, rep from * to end.

Join in B.

Rounds 5–12: Using B, *k1, p1, rep from * to end.

Now work in st st (knit every round) working stripes as folls:

1 round B
3 rounds A
1 round B
2 rounds A
7 rounds C
1 round A
2 rounds B
3 rounds C
1 round A
3 rounds B
10 rounds C

Round 35: Using C, k1, k2togtbl, k to last 3 sts, k2tog, k1. *58 sts*

1 round C
3 rounds A
2 rounds C
1 round A
2 rounds C

Round 45: Using C, k1, k2togtbl, k to last 3 sts, k2tog, k1. *56 sts*

10 rounds C

Shape heel

Slip first 14 sts and last 14 sts of last round onto one needle (for heel), and rem 28 sts onto holders (for top of foot).

With RS facing, join B to 28 heel sts. Now working backwards and forwards in rows, not rounds, work on these 28 sts only for heel as folls:

Starting with a knit row, work in st st for 12 rows, ending after a WS row.

Next row: K21, k2togtbl, turn.

Next row: P15, p2tog, turn.

Next row: K15, k2togtbl, turn.

Rep last 2 rows four more times, then first of these rows again, ending after a WS row. *16 sts*

Next row: K8 but do NOT turn. (Heel completed.)

Now working in rounds again, distributing sts evenly over 3 needles, start to shape foot as folls:

Next round: Using B, knit rem 8 sts of heel, using C, pick up and knit 6 sts down row-end edge of heel, k28, pick up and knit 6 sts up other row-end edge of heel, using B knit first 8 heel sts. *56 sts*

Using C, work 43 rounds.

Break off C, join in B and complete sock using B only.

Shape toe

Rounds 1–2: Knit.

Round 3: [K12, k2tog, k2togtbl, k12] twice. *52 sts*

Round 4: Knit.

Round 5: [K11, k2tog, k2togtbl, k11] twice. *48 sts*

Round 6: Knit.

Round 7: [K10, k2tog, k2togtbl, k10] twice. *44 sts*

Round 8: Knit.

Round 9: [K9, k2tog, k2togtbl, k9] twice. *40 sts*

Round 10: Knit.

Round 11: [K8, k2tog, k2togtbl, k8] twice. *36 sts*

Round 12: Knit.

Round 13: [K7, k2tog, k2togtbl, k7] twice. *32 sts*

Round 14: Knit.

Break yarn.

Slip first and last 8 sts onto one needle, and rem 16 sts onto another needle. Graft together sts from both needles to close toe.

TO MAKE UP

Weave in ends neatly, then press carefully.

A staple but stylish work favourite for men is best when knitted in a lovely soft yarn that is silky to the touch. This yarn has a light sheen that gives it a dressed up, city feel. The colours can easily be changed to create a bolder or subtler look.

Size
Approx 24cm from toe to heel

Yarn
One 50g ball of Rowan RYC Bamboo Soft in each of grey (A), pink (B) and two balls in taupe (C)

Needles
Set of 4 double-pointed 3.75mm knitting needles

Other materials
Stitch holder
Knitter's sewing needle

Tension
30 rows and 25 stitches to 10cm square over st st using 3.75mm needles

Abbreviations
See page 109

These socks are a favourite of mine – perfect for dressing up with a pair of heels and a tea dress or a trench coat. If you can change the buttons to match your shoes then your socks will run that extra mile for you. Although these lacy button socks are knitted in wool they will also work well in summer, knitted in a cotton yarn.

Size
Approx 20cm from heel to toe

Yarn
Two 50g balls of Rowan Pure Wool
DK in black

Needles
Pair of 3mm knitting needles

Other materials
Stitch holders
Knitter's sewing needle
4 small buttons
Sewing needle and thread

Tension
25 stitches and 35 rows to
10cm square over lace patt using
3mm needles

Abbreviations
See page 109

Lacy button socks

lace patt

Row 1: K2, *yo, skpo, k5, k2tog, yo, k1, rep from * to last st, k1.
Row 2 and foll 6 alt rows: Purl.
Row 3: K3, *yo, skpo, k3, k2tog, yo, k3, rep from * to end.
Row 5: K4, *yo, skpo, k1, k2tog, yo, k5, rep from *, ending last rep, k4.
Row 7: K5, *yo, sl 1, k2tog, psso, yo, k7, rep from *, ending last rep, k5.
Row 9: K4, *k2tog, yo, k1, yo, skpo, k5, rep from *, ending last rep, k4.
Row 11: K3, *k2tog, yo, k3, yo, skpo, k3, rep from * to end.
Row 13: K2, *k2tog, yo, k5, yo, skpo, k1, rep from * to last st, k1.
Row 15: K1, k2tog, yo, k7,*yo, sl 1, k2tog, psso, yo, k7, rep from * to last 3 sts, yo, skpo, k1.
Row 16: Purl.
These 16 rows form lace patt and are repeated.

right sock

Cast on 49 sts.
Knit 2 rows.
Row 3 (RS): K2, yo, k2tog, k to end.
Knit 3 rows.
Rep last 4 rows once more.
Row 11: Cast off 6 sts, then work lace patt starting with row 1 (the stitch on the right-hand needle counts as the first knit stitch).
Cont until 40 rows of lace patt have been completed.
Next row: Patt 23 sts, turn, place rem 20 sts on stitch holder.
Cont in patt until 75 rows of lace patt in total have been completed.
Knit 1 row.
Shape toe
Work in st st, starting with a knit row.
Dec 1 st at each end of next and every alt row until 13 sts rem.
Work 1 row.
Cast off.

Shape heel
Rejoin yarn to 20 sts on stitch holder. With right side facing, knit 1 row, inc 1 st at each end and 1 st in the centre.
23 sts
Work 11 rows st st without shaping.
**Next row: K14, k2tog, turn, *sl 1 purlwise, p5, p2tog, turn, sl 1 knitwise, k5, k2tog, turn, rep from * until 7 sts rem.
Next row: K7, pick up and knit 8 sts down heel.
Next row: P15, pick up and purl 8 sts down other side of heel.
Cont in st st until work measures same as top of sock to start of toe shaping.
Shape toe
Work in st st, starting with a knit row.
Dec 1 st at each end of next and every alt row until 13 sts rem.
Work 1 row.
Cast off.**

left sock

Cast on 49 sts.
Knit 1 row.
Row 2: K2, yo, k2tog, k to end.
Knit 3 rows.
Rep last 4 rows once more.
Row 10: Cast off 6 sts, k to end.
Work 40 rows of lace patt.
Next row: K20, patt 23 sts.
Next row: P23, turn, place rem 20 sts on stitch holder.
Cont in patt until 75 rows of lace patt in total have been completed.
Knit 1 row.
Shape toe
Work in st st, starting with a knit row.
Dec 1 st at each end of next and every alt row until 13 sts rem.
Work 1 row.
Cast off.
Shape heel
Rejoin yarn to 20 sts on stitch holder. With wrong side facing, purl 1 row, inc

1 st at each end and 1 st in the centre.
23 sts
Work 10 rows st st without shaping.
Work as for Right Sock from ** to **
to complete.

TO MAKE UP
Join foot and side seams neatly. Sew
two buttons to garter stitch cuff to align
with eyelet buttonholes.

Winter flower socks

pattern (both alike)

Using A, cast on 62 sts.

Rib row 1: K2, *p2, k2, rep from *
to end.

Rib row 2: P2, *k2, p2, rep from *
to end.

These 2 rows form the rib.

Cont in rib, working 2 rows A, 2 rows
B, 4 rows A, 2 rows E, 2 rows D, 2
rows E, 4 rows C, 2 rows D, 6 rows C.
Starting with a k row, cont in patt.

Row 1: Using E, k to end.

Row 2: Using E, p to end.

Row 3: K2E, *2D, 2E; rep from *
to end.

Row 4: P2E, *2D, 2E; rep from *
to end.

Row 5: K2E, *2D, 2E; rep from *
to end.

Row 6: Using E, p to end.

Row 7: Using E, k to end.

Row 8: Using A, p to end.

Row 9: Using A, k to end.

Rows 10–11: As rows 8–9.

Rows 12–24: Work from Chart 1. (Note
that 1st row of Chart is a purl row.)

Row 25: Using A, k to end.

Row 26: Using A, p to end.

Rows 27–28: As rows 25–26.

Row 29: Using E, k to end.

Row 30: Using E, p to end.

Row 31: K2E, *2D, 2E; rep from *
to end.

Row 32: P2E, *2D, 2E; rep from *
to end.

Row 33: K2E, *2D, 2E; rep from *
to end.

Row 34: Using E, p to end.

Row 35: Using E, k to end.

Row 36: Using C, p to end.

Row 37: Using C, k to end.

Rows 38–39: As rows 36–37.

Rows 40–52: Work from Chart 2. (Note
that 1st row of Chart is a purl row.)

Row 53: Using C, k to end.

Row 54: Using C, p to end.

Rows 55–56: As rows 53–54.

These 56 rows form the patt.

Work a further 24 rows in patt.

Divide for foot

Next row: Using A, k4, cast off next 15
sts, k next 23 sts, cast off next 15 sts,
k rem 3 sts.

Work on last set of 4 sts.

Starting with a p row, work 15 rows st st.

Break yarn.

Muted blues and browns give a distinct 'winter warming' feel to this pair of long, flower-motif socks. The pattern has a leg seam so that the motifs can be worked in intarsia. On cold winter evenings these are the perfect cosy socks to knit and to wear.

Size
Approx 22cm from toe to heel
and 35cm long

Yarn
Approx 75g of Jaeger
Matchmaker Merion 4ply in dark
blue (A), 25g in light blue (B), 75g
in cream (C), 25g in dark brown
(D) and 25g in tan (E)

Needles
Pair of 3mm knitting needles

Other materials
Stitch holder
Knitter's sewing needle

Tension
36 rows and 30 sts to
10cm square over patt using
3mm needles

Abbreviations
See page 109

WINTER FLOWER SOCKS

Chart 1

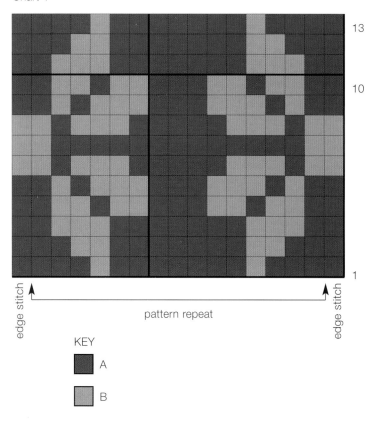

13

10

1

edge stitch

pattern repeat

edge stitch

KEY

A

B

Chart 2

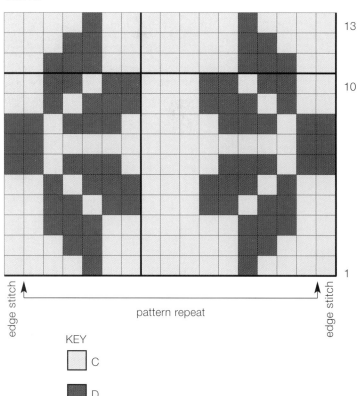

13

10

1

edge stitch

pattern repeat

edge stitch

KEY

C

D

With RS facing and A, pick up and k15 sts up right side of heel, k4. *19 sts*
Starting with a p row, work 14 rows st st. Break yarn.
Leave these sts on a holder.
Return to first set of 4 sts
Using A and starting with a p row, work 15 rows st st.
Next row: K4, pick up and k 15 sts down left side of heel. *19 sts*
Starting with a p row, work 14 rows st st.
Next row: Using A, p19, p across 24 sts of upper foot, p19 from second half of heel. *62 sts*
Work patt rows 27–56, then work rows 1–11.
Cont in patt.
Shape toe
Only work motifs that will come at centre of sole and centre of upper foot.
Row 1: Patt to end.
Row 2: Patt 13, k2tog, k2, skpo, patt 24, k2tog, k2, skpo, patt 13.
Row 3: Patt to end.
Row 4: Patt 12, k2tog, k2, skpo, patt 22, k2tog, k2, skpo, patt 12.
Row 5: Patt to end.
Row 6: Patt 11, k2tog, k2, skpo, patt 20, k2tog, k2, skpo, patt 11.
Cont in this way, dec on the 3 foll alt rows. *38 sts*
Purl 1 row.
Cont in A only.
Dec as set on next and 2 foll alt rows. *26 sts*
Purl 1 row.
Cast off.

TO MAKE UP
Weave in ends, then press carefully. Join cast off sts of leg section to sides of heel. Join back and sole seam. With seam at centre of foot, join toe seam.

Luscious legwarmers

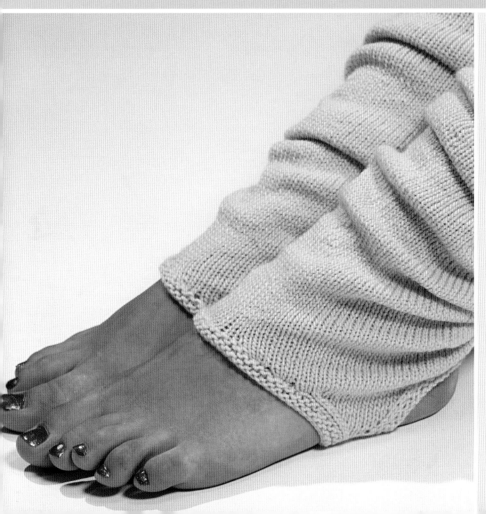

Bow legwarmers
Dog's legwarmers
Stirrup legwarmers
Sparkly legwarmers

Bows are a favourite of mine so it was essential to include these intarsia bow legwarmers in this book. The bows look striking in white on black, but will also look really cute in all kinds of girlie and bright colours. Alternatively, for a more grown-up look try them in chocolate brown with caramel coloured bows.

Bow legwarmers

pattern (both alike)

Using A, cast on 36 sts.

Distribute these sts evenly over 3 of the double-pointed needles and, using 4th needle, work in rounds as folls:

Round 1: Using A, *k2, p2, rep from * to end.

Rounds 2–3: As round 1.

Join in B.

Round 4: Using B, *k2, p2, rep from * to end.

Rounds 5–8: As round 1.

Round 9: As round 4.

Break off B.

Rounds 10–12: As round 1.

Round 13: K2, [inc in next st, k3] eight times, inc in next st, k1. *45 sts*

Rounds 14–18: Knit.

Round 19: K1, inc in next st, knit to last 3 sts, inc in next st, k2. *47 sts*

Rounds 20–37: Rep rounds 14–19 three more times. *53 sts*

Rounds 38–72: Knit.

Place bow chart

Using a separate length of yarn for each row of sts in B and stranding A across back of work, weaving yarns in on WS, place bow chart as folls:

Round 73: K16A, work next 21 sts as row 1 of bow chart, k16A.

This round sets position of chart.

Work a further 25 rounds, thereby completing all 26 rows of bow chart.

Cont using A only as folls:

Rounds 99–107: Knit.

Round 108: K2, k2tog, [k4, k2tog] eight times, k1. *44 sts*

Now rep rounds 1–12 once more.

Cast off in rib.

TO MAKE UP

Weave in ends neatly, then press carefully.

Size
Approx 16cm around ankle and approx 24cm around calf

Yarn
Two 50g balls of Jaeger Matchmaker Merino DK in black (A) and one ball in white (B)

Needles
Set of 4 double-pointed 4mm knitting needles

Other materials
Knitter's sewing needle

Tension
30 rows and 22 stitches to 10cm square over st st using 4mm needles

Abbreviations
See page 109

BOW LEGWARMERS

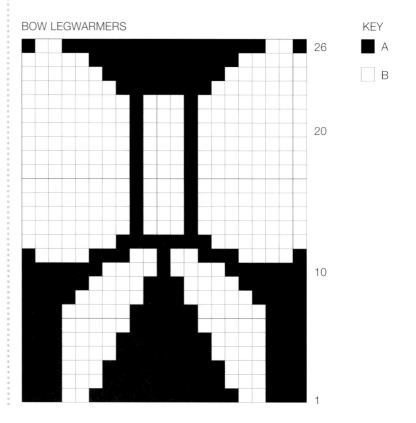

KEY

■ A

□ B

Dog's legwarmers

pattern (both alike)

Using 3.25mm needles, cast on 30 sts.

Row 1: *K1, p1, rep from * to end.

Rep row 1 seven more times.

Change to 4mm needles.

Starting with a k row, work 42 rows st st, ending with a p row.

Next row: K5, *k2tog, k4, rep from * to last 7 sts, k2tog, k5.

Next row: *K1, p1, rep from * to end.

Rep this last row thirteen more times.

Cast off in rib.

TO MAKE UP

Weave in ends neatly, then press carefully. Sew back seam neatly.

Collar bow

Main piece

Using 3.25mm needles, cast on 11 sts.

Row 1: Knit.

Row 2: K1, p to last st, k1.

Row 3: K1, [M1, k2] five times. *16 sts*

**Row 4: K1, p to last st, k1.

Row 5: Knit.

Row 6: K1, p to last st, k1.

Rows 7–22: Rep the last 2 rows eight more times.

Row 23: K1, [k2tog, k1] five times. *11 sts*

Row 24: K1, p to last st, k1.

Row 25: Knit.

Row 26: K1, p to last st, k1.**

Row 27: K1, [M1, k2] five times. *16 sts*

Rep from ** to ** once more.

Cast off.

Centre piece

Using 3.25mm needles, cast on 4 sts.

Row 1: Knit.

Row 2: K1, p to last st, k1.

Rep the last 2 rows until piece measures 6cm, ending with a row 2.

Cast off.

TO MAKE UP

Sew cast on and cast off edges of main piece together. Place seam to centre back of main piece. Wrap centre piece around middle of main piece, sew cast on and cast off edges together.

Not one to be missed out. Valentine the dog also wanted some legwarmers as she does get cold in winter. These legwarmers are the simplest project in the book and can easily be made bigger by casting on more stitches and knitting more rows.

Size
Approx 21cm long and 13.5cm around leg

Yarn
One 100g ball of Robin double knitting in fluorescent pink

Needles
Pair each of 3.25mm and 4mm knitting needles

Other materials
Knitter's sewing needle

Tension
30 rows and 22 sts to 10cm square over st st using 4mm needles

Abbreviations
See page 109

"Valentine wanted some legwarmers as she does get cold in winter. "

Stirrup legwarmers

pattern (both alike)

Cast on 72 sts.

Distribute these sts evenly over 3 of the double-pointed needles and, using 4th needle, work in rounds as folls:

Round 1: *K1, p1, rep from * to end.

Rep the last round nine more times.

Next round: Knit.

This round forms the st st

Cont in st st until until legwarmer measures 36cm from cast on edge.

Shape stirrups

**Next row: K36, turn and work back and forth in rows, not rounds, on these 36 sts.

Next row: Purl.

Cont in st st.

Next row: Cast off 4 sts, k to end.

Next row: Cast off 4 sts, p to end.

Next row: Cast off 3 sts, k to end.

Next row: Cast off 3 sts, p to end.

Next row: Cast off 2 sts, k to end.

Next row: Cast off 2 sts, p to end. *18 sts*

Next row: K1, skpo, k to last 3 sts, k2tog, k1.

Next row: Purl.

Rep the last 2 rows five more times.

Work a further 12 rows in st st (1 row knit, 1 row purl).

Cast off. **

With right side facing rejoin yarn to rem sts.

Work from ** to **.

Edgings (alike)

With RS facing, pick up and knit 50 sts from cast off edge to cast off edge.

Knit 3 rows.

Cast off.

TO MAKE UP

Weave in ends, then press carefully.

Join cast off edges and row ends.

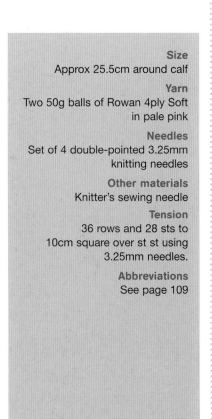

Size
Approx 25.5cm around calf

Yarn
Two 50g balls of Rowan 4ply Soft in pale pink

Needles
Set of 4 double-pointed 3.25mm knitting needles

Other materials
Knitter's sewing needle

Tension
36 rows and 28 sts to 10cm square over st st using 3.25mm needles.

Abbreviations
See page 109

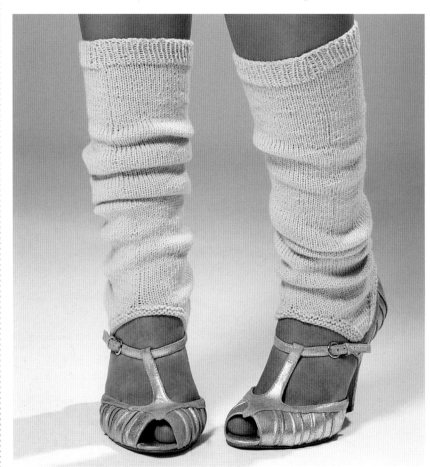

Sparkly legwarmers

pattern (both alike)

Using A, cast on 52 sts.

Distribute these sts evenly over 3 of the double-pointed needles and, using 4th needle, work in rounds as folls:

Round 1: *K1, p1, rep from * to end.

Rep this round forty-nine more times.

Join in B.

Rounds 51–58: Knit in B.

Round 59: Using A, [k24, k2tog] twice. *50 sts*

Rounds 60–64: Knit in A.

Round 65: Using A, [k23, k2tog] twice. *48 sts*

Round 66: Knit in A.

Join in C.

Rounds 67–70: Knit in C.

Round 71: Using C, [k22, k2tog] twice. *46 sts*

Rounds 72–74: Knit in C.

Rounds 75–76: Knit in B.

Round 77: Using B, [k21, k2tog] twice. *44 sts*

Rounds 78–82: Knit in B.

Round 83: Using A, [k20, k2tog] twice. *42 sts*

Rounds 84–90: Knit in A.

Rounds 91–98: Knit in C.

Rounds 99–106: Knit in B.

Break off B.

Rounds 107–114: Knit in A.

Rounds 115–122: Knit in C.

Break off C and cont using A only.

Round 123: [K6, inc in next st] six times. *48 sts*

Rounds 124–133: As round 1.

Cast off in rib.

TO MAKE UP

Weave in ends neatly, then press carefully.

In soft kid mohair with lurex these legwarmers have a distinctly 80s feel. They are quite slimfitting and look great worn with skinny jeans. If you add another stripe section (one stripe of each colour) you'll be able to pull them up to your thighs — very sexy!

Size
Approx 22cm around ankle and 27cm around calf

Yarn
One 25g ball of Rowan Kidsilk Haze (used double) in each of jade (A), camel (B) and black (C)
One spool of lurex sewing thread in each of silver and gold

Needles
Set of 4 double-pointed 4.5mm knitting needles

Other materials
Knitter's sewing needle

Tension
22 rows and 19 stitches to 10cm square over st st using 4.5mm knitting needles

Note
Use mohair yarn AND lurex thread held together throughout. Use silver lurex thread with jade yarn, and gold lurex thread with both camel and black yarn. Note that no reference is made to lurex thread in pattern.

Kid's stuff

Pink bootees

Spotty baby socks

Picot sandals

Stripy socks

Pink bootees

pattern (both alike)

Cast on 43 sts.

Row 1: Inc, k19, inc, k1, inc, k19, inc. *47 sts*

Rows 2–4: Knit.

Row 5: Inc, k21, inc, k1, inc, k21, inc. *51 sts*

Rows 6–7: Knit.

Starting with a k row, work 6 rows st st.

Shape instep

Next row: K21, [p1, k1] four times, skpo, turn.

Next row: P1, [k1, p1] four times, p2tog, turn.

Next row: K1, [p1, k1] four times, skpo, turn.

Rep last two rows six more times, then knit to end on last row without turning.

Cuff

Next row: P14, [k1, p1] four times, p14.

Next row: K14, [p1, k1] four times, k14.

Rep last two rows once more.

Next row: P14, [k1, p1] four times, p14.

Next row (eyelet row): K3, yo, k2tog, [k4, yo, k2tog] twice, k1, p1, k1, yo, k2tog, [k4, yo, k2tog] twice, k2. *36 sts*

Next row: P14, [k1, p1] four times, p14.

Next row: K14, put rem sts on holder. Working on these 14 sts, work 4 rows st st.

Cast off.

Rejoin yarn to moss section, leaving 14 sts of st st section on holder. Keeping moss patt correct, work 4 rows.

Next row: Skpo, moss 4, k2tog.

Next row: Skpo, moss 2, p2tog.

Cast off.

Rejoin yarn to rem 14 sts.

Work 5 rows st st.

Cast off.

TO MAKE UP

Weave in any loose ends. Using mattress stitch, sew underfoot and heel seam, reversing seam on last few rows of back. Thread ribbon through eyelets and tie in bow on front.

Size
One size to fit 12–18 months

Yarn
Two 25g hanks of Debbie Bliss Pure Cashmere in pink

Needles
Pair of 4mm knitting needles

Other materials
Stitch holder
Knitter's sewing needle
Two 50-cm long pieces of 7-mm wide satin ribbon

Tension
24 rows and 20 stitches to 10cm square over stocking stitch using 4mm needles

Abbreviations
See page 109

Spotty baby socks

pattern (both alike)

Using A, cast on 24 sts loosely.
Distribute these sts evenly over 3 of the double-pointed needles and, using 4th needle, work in rounds as folls:

Rounds 1–7: Knit.

Join in B.

Stranding yarn not in use loosely across WS of work, cont as folls:

Rounds 8–9: *K2B, k2A, rep from * to end.

Rounds 10–11: Knit in A.

Rounds 12–23: Rep rounds 8–11 three more times.

Shape heel

Next round: K12C, cast on 12 sts.
Slip rem 12 sts of main section onto a holder and distribute these 24 sts in C evenly over 3 of the double-pointed needles. Using 4th needle and C, work in rounds as folls:

**Next round: (Skpo, k7, k2tog, k1) twice. *20 sts*

Next round: (Skpo, k5, k2tog, k1) twice. *16 sts*

Next round: (Skpo, k3, k2tog, k1) twice. *12 sts*

Next round: (Skpo, k1, k2tog, k1) twice. *8 sts*

Next round: (Skpo, k2tog) twice. *4 sts*
Break yarn and thread through rem 4 sts. Pull up tightly and fasten off securely.**

Shape foot

Return to sts of main section and, with RS facing and using A, pick up and 12 sts from cast-on edge of heel, k rem 12 sts of main section. *24 sts*
Distribute these sts evenly over 3 of the double-pointed needles and, using 4th needle, work in rounds as folls:

Next round: Knit in A.
Rep rounds 8–11 three more times.
Break off B and cont using A only.

Next round: Knit in A.
Rep last round once more.

Shape toe

Work as for heel from ** to **.

TO MAKE UP
Weave in ends neatly, then press carefully.

You will know that your baby's feet are snuggly in these lovely square-spot sockettes. In a chunky yarn and with the right tension the socks should be able to be worn over a six-month period as they will stretch nicely.

"Your baby's feet will be really snuggly in these cute sockettes."

Size
Approx 11cm from toe to heel

Yarn
One 50g ball of Debbie Bliss Rialto Aran in each of blue (A), peach (B) and white (C)

Needles
Set of 4 double-pointed 4.5mm knitting needles

Other materials
Stitch holders
Knitter's sewing needle

Tension
25 rows and 19 stitches to 10cm square over patt using 4.5mm needles

Abbreviations
See page 109

These sweet baby shoes with ankle straps are perfect dressing up shoes for little darlings. I've used a cotton yarn to give the shoes a summer feel and added a contrast colour button for extra interest.

Picot sandals

left sandal

**Sole

Cast on 32 sts.

Row 1: [K1, inc, k12, inc, k1] rep once more.

Row 2 and alt rows: Knit.

Row 3: [K1, inc, k14, inc, k1] rep once more.

Row 5: [K1, inc, k16, inck1] rep once more.

Row 7: [K1, inc, k18, inc, k1] rep once more.

Row 9: [K1, inc, k20, inc, k1] rep once more. *52 sts*

Rows 10–15: Knit.

Shape instep

Row 16: K30, turn.

Rows 17–33: K7, skpo, turn. *35 sts*

Row 34: K7, skpo, k13.

Rows 35–37: Knit across all sts.

Row 38: Cast off 7 sts, *slip st on right-hand needle onto left-hand needle, cast on 3 sts, cast off 5 sts*, rep from * to * nine more times, cast off rem sts.

Ankle strap

Join heel and underfoot seam.

Cast on 10 sts, with RS facing pick up and knit 12 sts from heel (6 sts each side of heel seam), cast on 10 sts.

Row 1: Knit.**

Row 2: Knit to last 4 sts, k2tog, yo, k2.

Row 3: Knit.

Row 4: Cast off 4 sts, *slip st on right-hand needle onto left-hand needle, cast on 3 sts, cast off 5 sts*, rep from * to * eleven more times, cast off rem sts.

right sandal

Work as for Left Sandal from ** to **.

Row 2: K2, yo, k2tog, knit to end.

Row 3: Knit.

Row 4: Cast off 4 sts, *slip st on right-hand needle onto left-hand needle, cast on 3 sts, cast off 5 sts*, rep from * to * eleven more times, cast off rem sts.

TO MAKE UP

Weave in any loose ends. Sew buttons onto ends of ankle straps to align with buttonholes.

Size
One size to fit 0–3 months

Yarn
One 50g ball of Rowan Cotton Glacé in cream

Needles
Pair of 3.25mm knitting needles

Other materials
Knitter's sewing needle
Sewing needle and thread
2 small buttons

Tension
52 rows and 26 stitches to 10cm square over garter stitch using 3.25mm needles

Abbreviations
See page 109

"Perfect dressing up shoes for little darlings. "

"Bright colours will work best for kids' fun socks."

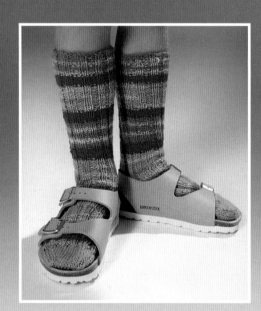

Stripy socks

pattern

Using A, cast on 44 sts.

Distribute these sts evenly over 3 of the double-pointed needles and, using 4th needle, work in rounds as folls:

Left sock

Round 1: *P2, k2, rep from * to end.

Right sock

Round 1: *K2, p2, rep from * to end.

Both socks

This round forms rib.

Keeping rib correct and joining in colours as required, cont in stripes as folls:

Rounds 2–3: Using A.

Rounds 4–6: Using B.

Rounds 7–9: Using A.

Rounds 10–12: Using B.

Rounds 13–18: Using C.

Rounds 19–21: Using B.

Rounds 22–24: Using D.

Rounds 25–27: Using B.

Rounds 28–30: Using D.

Rounds 31–33: Using B.

Rounds 34–39: Using C.

Rounds 40–42: Using A.

Rounds 43–45: Using B.

Rounds 46–48: Using A.

Rounds 49–51: Using B.

Rounds 52–54: Using A.

Rounds 55–61: Using C.

Rounds 62–64: Using D.

Rounds 65–68: Using B.

Rounds 69–71: Using D.

Rounds 72–74: Using B.

Rounds 75–77: Using D.

Shape heel

Left sock

Slip first 22 sts onto holders.

Right sock

Slip last 22 sts onto holders.

Both socks

Rejoin C to rem 22 sts.

Working backwards and forwards in rows, not rounds, work on these 22 sts only for heel as folls:

Row 1: K21, wrap next st, turn.

Row 2: P20, wrap next st, turn.

Row 3: K19, wrap next st, turn.

Row 4: P18, wrap next st, turn.

Row 5: K17, wrap next st, turn.

Row 6: P16, wrap next st, turn.

Row 7: K15, wrap next st, turn.

Row 8: P14, wrap next st, turn.

Row 9: K13, wrap next st, turn.

Row 10: P12, wrap next st, turn.

Row 11: K11, wrap next st, turn.

Row 12: P10, wrap next st, turn.

Row 13: K11, turn.

Row 14: P12, turn.

Row 15: K13, turn.

Row 16: P14, turn.

Row 17: K15, turn.

Row 18: P16, turn.

Row 19: K17, turn.

Row 20: P18, turn.

Row 21: K19, turn.

Row 22: P20, turn.

Row 23: K21, turn.

Row 24: P22.

Break off C. (Heel completed.)

Distribute all 44 sts over 3 needles and work in rounds, starting at end of last complete round worked, as folls:

Left sock

Next round: Using B, rib 22, k22.

Right sock

Next round: Using B, k22, rib 22.

Both socks

Last round sets position of rib on top of foot and st st on sole.

Keeping sts correct as now set, cont in stripes as folls:

Using B, work 3 rounds.

My friend Sophie's Mum. Sal. used to knit hundreds of stripy pairs of socks like these and gave them to almost everyone she knew. Bright colours will work best for kids and the recipient will have a fun pair of socks they'll remember.

Size
Approx 18cm from toe to heel

Yarn
One 50g ball of Regia 4 ply in each of blue (A), beige (B), pink (C) and green (D)

Needles
Set of 4 double-pointed 3mm knitting needles

Other materials
Stitch holder
Knitter's sewing needle

Tension
42 rows and 30 stitches to 10cm square over st st using 4mm needles

Abbreviations
See page 109

Using A, work 5 rounds.
Using B, work 5 rounds.
Using C, work 4 rounds.
Using B, work 5 rounds.
Using D, work 5 rounds.
Using B, work 5 rounds.
Using A, work 4 rounds.
Using B, work 4 rounds.
Using C, work 4 rounds.
Using B, work 4 rounds.
Break off A, B and C and cont
using D only.

Shape toe

Rounds 1–2: Knit.
Round 3: (K1, k2togtbl, k16, k2tog, k1)
twice. *40 sts*
Round 4: Knit.
Round 5: (K1, k2togtbl, k14, k2tog, k1)
twice. *36 sts*
Round 6: Knit.
Round 7: (K1, k2togtbl, k12, k2tog, k1)
twice. *32 sts*
Round 8: Knit.
Round 9: (K1, k2togtbl, k10, k2tog, k1)
twice. *28 sts*
Round 10: Knit.
Round 11: (K1, k2togtbl, k8, k2tog, k1)
twice. *24 sts*
Round 12: Knit.
Break yarn, leaving a long end.
Slip first 12 sts onto one needle, and
last 12 sts onto another needle.
Using long end left at toe, graft together
sts from both needles to close toe.

TO MAKE UP
Weave in ends neatly, then press
carefully.

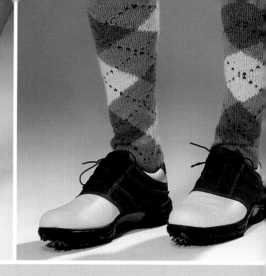

Outdoor socks

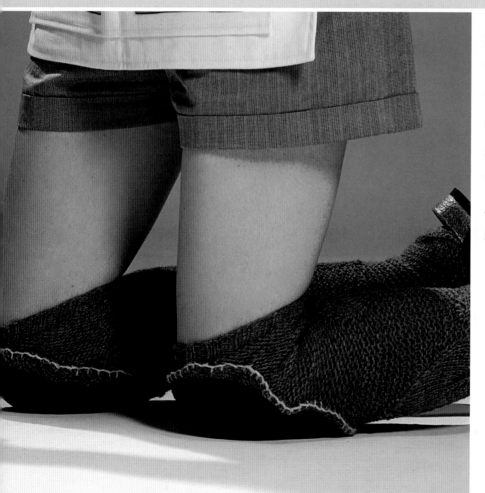

Lace-cuff wellie socks

Walk-the-dog socks

Tennis socks

Gardening long socks

Ski socks

Men's Aran wellie socks

Argyle golf socks

Striped football socks

It's so annoying to lose your socks inside your wellies so I've designed these socks with cuffs that turn over the top of the boots, and you can easily push your jeans inside the socks. I've embellished them with satin ribbon and beads to match the hot-pink wellies.

Lace-cuff wellie socks

Size
Approx 23cm from toe to heel

Yarn
Three 50g balls of Garthenor 100% Organic Shetland in oatmeal

Needles
Set of 4 double-pointed 3.25mm knitting needles

Other materials
Cable needle
Stitch holder
Knitter's sewing needle
1m of narrow ribbon
Four 1.5cm round beads

Tension
36 rows and 28 stitches to 10cm square over st st using 3.25mm needles

Abbreviations
See page 109
Cr3R = slip next 2 sts onto cable needle and leave at front of work, p1, then p2 from cable needle
Cr3L = slip next st onto cable needle and leave at back of work, p2, then p1 from cable needle

pattern (both alike)

Cast on 104 sts.
Distribute these sts evenly over 3 of the double-pointed needles and, using 4th needle, work in rounds as folls:
Round 1: *P2, sl 1, p3, sl 1, p1, rep from * to end.
Now work in patt as folls:
Round 2: *P2, sl 1, p3, sl 1, p1, rep from * to end.
Round 3: *Cr3R, p1, sl 1, p1, p1 enclosing loops of previous 2 rounds in st, p1, rep from * to end.
Round 4: *Sl 1, p3, rep from * to end.
Round 5: *Sl 1, p3, p1 enclosing loops of previous 2 rounds in st, p1, sl 1, p1, rep from * to end.
Round 6: *Cr3L, p3, sl 1, p1, rep from * to end.
Round 7: *P2, [sl 1, p1] twice, p1 enclosing loops of previous 2 rounds in st, p1, rep from * to end.
Round 8: *P2, sl 1, p1, sl 1, p3, rep from * to end.
Round 9: *Cr3R, p1, p1 enclosing loops of previous 2 rounds in st, p1, sl 1, p1, rep from * to end.
Round 10: *Sl 1, p5, sl 1, p1, rep from * to end.
Round 11: *Sl 1, p3, sl 1, p1, p1 enclosing loops of previous 2 rounds in st, p1, rep from * to end.
Round 12: *Cr3L, p1, sl 1, p3, rep from * to end.
Round 13: *P2, sl 1, p1, p1 enclosing loops of previous 2 rounds in st, p1, sl 1, p1, rep from * to end.
Rounds 2–13 form patt.
Cont in patt until sock measures 10cm. (Cuff completed.)
Next round: [K12, k2tog, k12] four times. *100 sts*
Next round: Knit.
Last round forms st st.
Work in st st for a further 8 rounds.
Place markers on needles after first and last 25 sts – 50 sts between markers.
Next round: *K to within 2 sts of marker, k2tog, slip marker onto right needle, k2togtbl, rep from * once more, knit to end. *96 sts*
Work 9 rounds.
Rep last 10 rounds nine more times. *60 sts*
Work a further 9 rounds.
Shape heel
Now working backwards and forwards in rows, not rounds, shape heel as folls:
Row 1: K14, wrap next st, turn.
Row 2: P28, wrap next st, turn.
Row 3: K27, wrap next st, turn.
Row 4: P26, wrap next st, turn.
Row 5: K25, wrap next st, turn.
Row 6: P24, wrap next st, turn.
Row 7: K23, wrap next st, turn.
Row 8: P22, wrap next st, turn.
Row 9: K21, wrap next st, turn.
Row 10: P20, wrap next st, turn.
Row 11: K19, wrap next st, turn.
Row 12: P18, wrap next st, turn.
Row 13: K17, wrap next st, turn.
Row 14: P16, wrap next st, turn.
Row 15: K17, turn.
Row 16: P18, turn.
Row 17: K19, turn.
Row 18: P20, turn.
Row 19: K21, turn.
Row 20: P22, turn.
Row 21: K23, turn.
Row 22: P24, turn.
Row 23: K25, turn.
Row 24: P26, turn.
Row 25: K27, turn.
Row 26: P28, turn.
Row 27: K29, turn.
Row 28: P30.
Row 29: K15 but do NOT turn. (Heel completed.)
Now working in rounds again, distributing sts evenly over 3 needles, start to shape foot as folls:
Next round: Knit.
Rep last round until foot measures 18cm from back of heel.

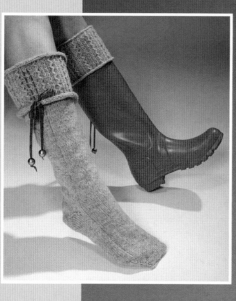

Shape toe

Round 1: [K13, k2tog, k2togtbl, k13] twice. *56 sts*

Round 2: Knit.

Round 3: [K12, k2tog, k2togtbl, k12] twice. *52 sts*

Round 4: Knit.

Round 5: [K11, k2tog, k2togtbl, k11] twice. *48 sts*

Round 6: Knit.

Round 7: [K10, k2tog, k2togtbl, k10] twice. *44 sts*

Round 8: Knit.

Round 9: [K9, k2tog, k2togtbl, k9] twice. *40 sts*

Round 10: Knit.

Round 11: [K8, k2tog, k2togtbl, k8] twice. *36 sts*

Round 12: Knit.

Round 13: [K7, k2tog, k2togtbl, k7] twice. *32 sts*

Round 14: Knit.

Break yarn.

Slip first and last 8 sts onto one needle, and rem 16 sts onto another needle. Graft together sts from both needles to close toe.

TO MAKE UP

Weave in ends neatly, then press carefully. Cut ribbon in half. Using photo as a guide and starting and ending at cast on edge, thread ribbon through sts of cuff in two parallel lines. Tie beads to ends of ribbon.

"You'll love walking your dog in these socks."

Walk-the-dog socks

left sock

Using A, cast on 52 sts.

Distribute these sts evenly over 3 of the double-pointed needles and, using 4th needle, work in rounds as folls:

Rounds 1–9: Knit.

Round 10: *Yo, k2tog, rep from * to end.

Rounds 11–19: Knit.

Round 20: Fold cast-on edge to inside and knit tog first st on left needle with first cast-on st, *k tog next st on left needle with next cast-on st, rep from * to end.

Break off A and join in B.

Round 21–24: Knit.

Place first and second motifs

Stranding yarn not in use loosely across WS of work, weaving it in every 3 or 4 sts, place charts as folls:

Round 25: Using B k6, work next 16 sts as row 1 of chart A, using B k8, work next 16 sts as row 1 of chart B, using B k6.

This round sets position of charts.

Work a further 19 rounds, thereby completing all 20 rows of charts.

Place third motif

Round 45: Using B k18, work next 16 sts as row 1 of chart A, using B k18. This round sets position of chart. Work a further 19 rounds, thereby completing all 20 rows of chart.

Place fourth and fifth motifs

Round 65: Using B k6, work next 16 sts as row 1 of chart B, using B k8, work next 16 sts as row 1 of chart A, using B k6.

This round sets position of charts. Keeping charts correct, work 7 rounds.

Round 73: K1, k2togtbl, patt to last 3 sts, k2tog, k1. *50 sts*

Work 9 rounds.

Round 83: As round 73. *48 sts*

Work 1 round, thereby completing all 20 rows of charts.

Place sixth motif

Round 85: Using B k16, work next 16 sts as row 1 of chart B, using B k16. This round sets position of chart.

Knitted in a gorgeous cashmere and merino blend yarn, you'll love walking your dog in these socks, even on the coldest of mornings. The cute doggie Fair Isle motif is complemented with a picot edge at the top of the sock.

WALK-THE-DOG SOCKS

Chart A

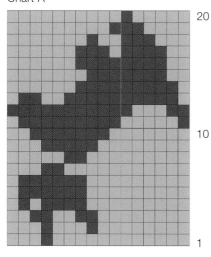

Chart B

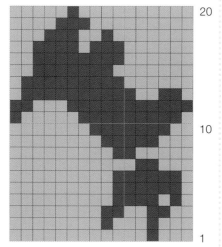

KEY
- ◻ A
- ◼ B

Size
Approx 22cm from toe to heel

Yarn
Two 50g balls of Debbie Bliss Cashmerino DK in each of grey (A) and green (B)

Needles
Set of 4 double-pointed 4mm knitting needles

Other materials
Stitch holder
Knitter's sewing needle

Tension
30 rows and 22 stitches to 10cm square over st st using 4mm needles

Abbreviations
See page 109

Work 5 rounds, ending after chart
row 6.
Break off B.

Shape heel

Slip first 12 sts and last 12 sts of
last round onto one needle (for heel),
and rem 24 sts onto holders (for top
of foot).

With RS facing, join A to 24 heel sts.
Now working backwards and forwards
in rows, not rounds, work on these 24
sts only for heel as folls:

Row 1: K23, wrap next st, turn.
Row 2: P22, wrap next st, turn.
Row 3: K21, wrap next st, turn.
Row 4: P20, wrap next st, turn.
Row 5: K19, wrap next st, turn.
Row 6: P18, wrap next st, turn.
Row 7: K17, wrap next st, turn.
Row 8: P16, wrap next st, turn.
Row 9: K15, wrap next st, turn.
Row 10: P14, wrap next st, turn.
Row 11: K13, wrap next st, turn.
Row 12: P12, wrap next st, turn.
Row 13: K11, wrap next st, turn.
Row 14: P10, wrap next st, turn.
Row 15: K11, turn.
Row 16: P12, turn.
Row 17: K13, turn.
Row 18: P14, turn.
Row 19: K15, turn.
Row 20: P16, turn.
Row 21: K17, turn.
Row 22: P18, turn.
Row 23: K19, turn.
Row 24: P20, turn.
Row 25: K21, turn.
Row 26: P22, turn.
Row 27: K23, turn.
Row 28: P24.
Break off A. (Heel completed.)
Distribute all 48 sts over 3 needles and,
starting and ending rounds at centre of
heel sts, now work in rounds as folls:
Next round: Using B k16, patt 16 sts of
chart, using B k16.
Keeping sts correct as now set, work a
further 13 rounds, thereby completing

all 20 rows of chart.
Next round: Using B, knit.
Rep last round twenty-four more times.
Break off B, join in A and complete
sock using A only.

Shape toe

Round 1: Knit.
Round 2: [K10, k2tog, k2togtbl, k10]
twice. *44 sts*
Round 3: Knit.
Round 4: [K9, k2tog, k2togtbl, k9]
twice. *40 sts*
Round 5: Knit.
Round 6: [K8, k2tog, k2togtbl, k8]
twice. *36 sts*
Round 7: Knit.
Round 8: [K7, k2tog, k2togtbl, k7]
twice. *32 sts*
Round 9: Knit.
Round 10: [K6, k2tog, k2togtbl, k6]
twice. *28 sts*
Round 11: Knit.
Round 12: [K5, k2tog, k2togtbl, k5]
twice. *24 sts*
Round 13: Knit.
Break yarn.
Slip first and last 6 sts onto one needle,
and last 12 sts onto another needle.
Graft together sts from both needles to
close toe.

right sock

Work as given for Left Sock, but
replacing chart A on round 45 with
chart B, and chart B on round 85 with
chart A.

TO MAKE UP
Weave in ends neatly, then press
carefully.

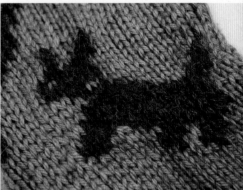

Tennis socks

pattern (both alike)

Using A, cast on 44 sts.

Distribute these sts evenly over 3 of the double-pointed needles and, using 4th needle, work in rounds as folls:

Rounds 1–6: Knit in A.

Round 7: Fold cast-on edge to inside and knit tog first st on left needle with first cast-on st, *k tog next st on left needle with next cast-on st, rep from * to end.

Break off A and complete sock using B.

Round 8–14: Knit.

Round 15: Fold cast-on edge to inside and knit tog first st on left needle with first st of second row knitted using B, *k tog next st on left needle with next st of second row knitted using B, rep from * to end.

Rounds 16–20: Knit.

Shape heel

Next row: K22, turn.

Slip rem 22 sts onto holders and working backwards and forwards in rows, not rounds, work on these 22 sts for heel as folls:

Starting with a purl row, work in st st for a further 9 rows, ending after a purl row.

Next row: K14, k2togtbl, turn.

Next row: P7, p2tog, turn.

Next row: K7, k2togtbl, turn.

Rep last 2 rows five more times, then first of these 2 rows again. *8 sts*

Break yarn.

Shape foot

With RS facing, rejoin yarn at beg of first row of heel and pick up and knit 7 sts up row-end edge of heel, knit 8 heel sts, then pick up and knit 7 sts down other row-end edge of heel, knit to end. *44 sts*

Distribute these sts evenly over 3 of the double-pointed needles and, using 4th needle, cont as folls:

Next round: Knit.

Rep this round sixteen more times.

Next round: *K2, p2, rep from * to end.

Rep this round thirteen more times.

Next round: Knit.

Rep last round twelve more times.

Shape toe

Round 1: Knit.

Round 2: [K1, k2togtbl, k16, k2tog, k1] twice. *40 sts*

Round 3: Knit.

Round 4: [K1, k2togtbl, k14, k2tog, k1] twice. *36 sts*

Round 5: Knit.

Round 6: [K1, k2togtbl, k12, k2tog, k1] twice. *32 sts*

Round 7: Knit.

Round 8: [K1, k2togtbl, k10, k2tog, k1] twice. *28 sts*

Round 9: Knit.

Round 10: [K1, k2togtbl, k8, k2tog, k1] twice. *24 sts*

Round 11: Knit.

Break yarn, leaving a long end.

Slip first 12 sts onto one needle, and last 12 sts onto another needle.

Using long end left at toe, graft together sts from both needles to close toe.

Bow strips

Using A, cast on 9 sts.

Distribute these sts evenly over 3 of the double-pointed needles and, using 4th needle, work in rounds as folls:

Round 1: Knit.

Rep this round until bow strip measures 25cm from cast on edge.

Cast off.

TO MAKE UP

Weave in ends neatly, then press carefully. Tie bow strips into bows and sew to back of heel as in photograph.

What a classic! These cute, traditional-style tennis socks have knitted pintucks at the ankles to make a double cuff. The pretty bow could easily be exchanged for pom-poms, or you could use satin or grosgrain ribbon instead of a knitted bow.

Size
Approx 22cm from toe to heel

Yarn
One 50g ball of Rowan Cotton Glace in pale blue (A) and two balls in white (B)

Needles
Set of 4 double-pointed 3.25mm knitting needles

Other materials
Stitch holder
Knitter's sewing needle
Sewing needle and thread

Tension
32 rows and 23 stitches to 10cm square over st st using 3.25mm needles

Abbreviations
See page 109

No more sore knees after a day of weeding. My gardening socks have extra padding at the knee: a layer of garter stitch knitting and a layer of leather, both hand-sewn to the sock. If you prefer not to use leather, two layers of heavy canvas will do the trick.

Size
Approx 23cm from toe to heel

Yarn
Three 100g balls of Sirdar Country Style DK in green
Small amount of DK in cream

Needles
Set of 4 double-pointed 3.75mm knitting needles
Pair of 4mm knitting needles

Other materials
Stitch holders
Knitter's sewing needle
20 x 30cm piece of soft leather
Paper for patch pattern
Scissors
Needle and sewing thread

Tension
37 rows and 22 stitches to 10cm square over garter stitch using 3.75mm needles

Abbreviations
See page 109

Gardening long socks

pattern (both alike)

Using 3.75mm needles, cast on 56 sts loosely.
Distribute these sts evenly over 3 of the double-pointed needles and, using 4th needle, work in rounds as folls:
Rounds 1–8: *K2, p2, rep from * to end.
Now shape for knee as folls:
Row 9: K52, wrap next st, turn.
Row 10: K48, wrap next st, turn.
Row 11: K44, wrap next st, turn.
Row 12: K40, wrap next st, turn.
Row 13: K36, wrap next st, turn.
Row 14: K32, wrap next st, turn.
Row 15: K28, wrap next st, turn.
Row 16: K24, wrap next st, turn.
Row 17: K20, wrap next st, turn.
Row 18: K16, wrap next st, turn.
Row 19: K12, wrap next st, turn.
Row 20: K8, wrap next st, turn.
Row 21: Knit to end.
Now working in rounds, cont as folls:
Round 22: Purl.
Round 23: Knit.
These 2 rounds form circular garter st. Cont in circular garter st until sock measures 33cm at beg of rounds (36cm at centre of rounds), ending after a purl row.
Next round: K1, k2tog, k to last 3 sts, k2togtbl, k1. *54 sts*
Cont in circular garter st until sock measures 43cm at beg of rounds (46cm at centre of rounds), ending after a purl row.
Next round: K1, k2tog, k to last 3 sts, k2togtbl, k1. *52 sts*
Cont in circular garter st until sock measures 48cm at beg of rounds (51cm at centre of rounds), ending after a purl row.
Break yarn.
Shape heel
Slip first 13 sts and last 13 sts of last round onto one needle and leave rem 26 sts on a holder.
Work on 26 sts on needle only for heel.

Rejoin yarn with RS facing and knit to end.
Starting with a purl row, work in st st for a further 11 rows on these 26 sts, ending after a purl row.
Next row: K17, k2togtbl, turn.
Next row: P9, p2tog, turn.
Next row: K9, k2togtbl, turn.
Rep last 2 rows six more times, then first of these 2 rows again. *10 sts*
Break yarn.
Shape foot
Left sock only
With RS facing, rejoin yarn at end of first row of heel, k26, then pick up and knit 8 sts up row-end edge of heel, knit 10 heel sts, and pick up and knit 8 sts down other row-end edge of heel.
52 sts
Right sock only
With RS facing, rejoin yarn at beg of first row of heel and pick up and knit 8 sts up row-end edge of heel, knit 10 heel sts, then pick up and knit 8 sts down other row-end edge of heel, knit to end. *52 sts*
Both socks
Distribute these sts evenly over 3 of the double-pointed needles and, using 4th needle, work in circular garter st (starting with a purl round) until work measures 18cm from back of heel, ending after a purl round.
Shape toe
Round 1: Knit.
Round 2: [K1, k2togtbl, k20, k2tog, k1] twice. *48 sts*
Round 3: Knit.
Round 4: [K1, k2togtbl, k18, k2tog, k1] twice. *44 sts*
Round 5: Knit.
Round 6: [K1, k2togtbl, k16, k2tog, k1] twice. *40 sts*
Round 7: Knit.
Round 8: [K1, k2togtbl, k14, k2tog, k1] twice. *36 sts*
Round 9: Knit.
Round 10: [K1, k2togtbl, k12, k2tog,

"These long gardening socks have extra padding at the knee."

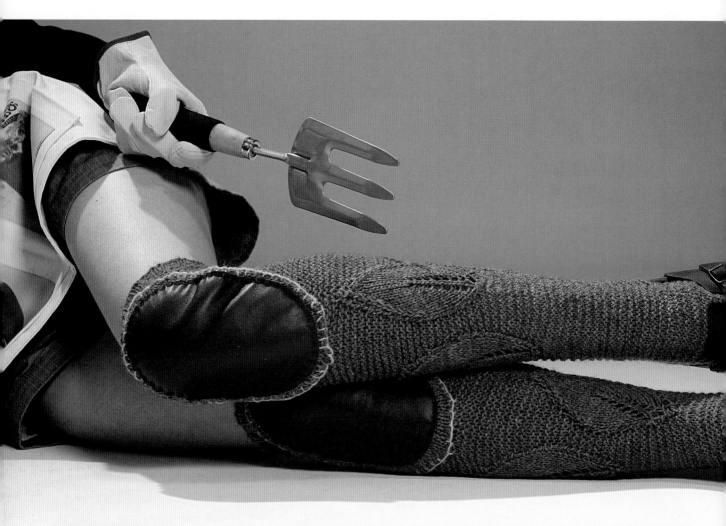

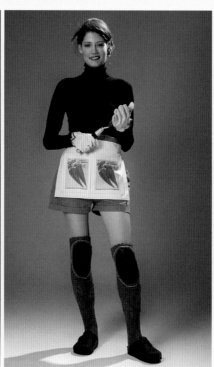
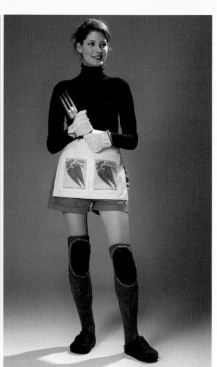

k1] twice. *32 sts*

Round 11: Knit.

Round 12: [K1, k2togtbl, k10, k2tog, k1] twice. *28 sts*

Round 13: Knit.

Break yarn, leaving a long end.

Slip first 14 sts onto one needle, and last 14 sts onto another needle.

Using long end left at toe, graft together sts from both needles to close toe.

Knee patches (make 2)

Using 4mm needles and doubled yarn, cast on 13 sts loosely.

Row 1: Knit.

Row 2: K1, M1, purl to last st, M1, k1.

Row 3: K1, M1, knit to last st, M1, k1.

Rows 4–9: As rows 2–3 three times. *29 sts*

Row 10: K1, purl to last st, k1.

Row 11: As row 3. *31 sts*

Row 12: As row 10.

Row 13: Knit.

Row 14: As row 10.

Row 15: As row 3. *33 sts*

Row 16: K1, purl to last st, k1.

Row 17: Knit.

Rows 18–41: As rows 16–17 twelve times.

Row 42: As row 16.

Row 43: K1, k2tog, k to last 3 sts, k2togtbl, k1. *31 sts*

Row 44: As row 16.

Row 45: Knit.

Row 46: As row 16.

Row 47: As row 43. *29 sts*

Row 48: As row 16.

Row 49: K1, k2tog, k to last 3 sts, k2togtbl, k1.

Row 50: K1, p2togtbl, purl to last 3 sts, p2tog, k1.

Rows 51–56: As rows 49–50 three times.

Cast off rem 13 sts.

Leaves (make 8)

Using 4mm needles, cast on 3 sts.

Row 1: [K1, yo] twice, k1. *5 sts*

Row 2 and every foll alt row: K1, purl to last st, k1.

Row 3: K2, yo, k1, yo, k2. *7 sts*

Row 5: K3, yo, k1, yo, k3. *9 sts*

Row 7: K4, yo, k1, yo, k4. *11 sts*

Row 9: K5, yo, k1, yo, k5. *13 sts*

Row 11: K6, yo, k1, yo, k6. *15 sts*

Row 13: K7, yo, k1, yo, k7. *17 sts*

Row 15: K8, yo, k1, yo, k8. *19 sts*

Row 17: K1, k2togtbl, k13, k2tog, k1. *17 sts*

Row 19: K1, k2togtbl, k11, k2tog, k1. *15 sts*

Row 21: K1, k2togtbl, k9, k2tog, k1. *13 sts*

Row 23: K1, k2togtbl, k7, k2tog, k1. *11 sts*

Row 25: K1, k2togtbl, k5, k2tog, k1. *9 sts*

Row 27: K1, k2togtbl, k3, k2tog, k1. *7 sts*

Row 29: K1, k2togtbl, k1, k2tog, k1. *5 sts*

Row 31: K1, sl 1, k2tog, psso, k1. *3 sts*

Row 33: Sl 1, k2tog, psso, fasten off.

TO MAKE UP

Weave in ends neatly, then press carefully.

Draw around knee patch and cut a paper pattern approx 1cm smaller all around. Use pattern to cut two patches from soft leather. Using sewing needle and thread, sew leather patches centrally to knitted patches.

Using photograph as a guide, sew knee patches onto knees using cream yarn and blanket stitch. Using main yarn and slip stitch, sew leaves at random over rest of sock.

Ski socks

left sock

Using A, cast on 48 sts.

Distribute these sts evenly over 3 of the double-pointed needles and, using 4th needle, work in rounds as folls:

Rounds 1–15: *K2, p2, rep from * to end.

Break off A and join in B.

Round 16: K11, M1, k1, M1, k36. *50 sts*

Rounds 17–60: Knit.

Round 61: K34, k2tog, k1, k2togtbl, k11. *48 sts*

Rounds 62–70: Knit.

Round 71: K33, k2tog, k1, k2togtbl, k10. *46 sts*

Rounds 72–80: Knit.

Shape heel

Next round: K23 and slip these 23 sts onto holders, join in A and using A knit rem 23 sts.

Now working backwards and forwards in rows, not rounds, work on these 23 sts only for heel as folls:

Starting with a purl row and using A, work in st st for a further 9 rows, ending after a purl row.

Next row: K16, k2togtbl, turn.

Next row: P10, p2tog, turn.

Next row: K10, k2togtbl, turn.

Rep last 2 rows four more times, then first of these 2 rows again. 11 sts

Break off A.

Shape foot

With RS facing, return to sts left on holders, using B knit these 23 sts, pick up and knit 6 sts up row-end edge of heel, knit 11 heel sts, then pick up and knit 6 sts down other row-end edge of heel. *46 sts*

**Distribute these sts evenly over 3 of the double-pointed needles and, using 4th needle, cont as folls:

Next round: Knit in B.

Rep this round forty-three more times. Break off B and cont using A only.

Shape toe

Rounds 1–2: Knit.

Round 3: [K1, k2togtbl, k17, k2tog, k1] twice. *42 sts*

Size
Approx 23cm from toe to heel

Yarn
One 50g ball of Rowan RYC Cashsoft DK in black (A) and two balls in orange (B)

Needles
Set of 4 double-pointed 4mm knitting needles

Other materials
Stitch holder
Knitter's sewing needle

Tension
30 rows and 22 stitches to 10cm square over st st using 4mm needles

Abbreviations
See page 109

I love a skull and crossbones motif so I've adapted it to include crossed skis for these socks. As a snowboarder, I know that a good pair of socks makes all the difference. Riding the mountain will be a joy in these cashmere-blend beauties.

SKI SOCKS

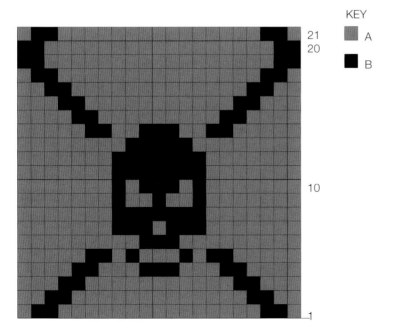

KEY

21
20

☒ A

■ B

10

1

Round 4: Knit.
Round 5: [K1, k2togtbl, k15, k2tog, k1] twice. *38 sts*
Round 6: Knit.
Round 7: [K1, k2togtbl, k13, k2tog, k1] twice. *34 sts*
Round 8: Knit.
Round 9: [K1, k2togtbl, k11, k2tog, k1] twice. *30 sts*
Round 10: Knit.
Round 11: [K1, k2togtbl, k9, k2tog, k1] twice. *26 sts*
Round 12: Knit.
Break yarn, leaving a long end.
Slip first 13 sts onto one needle, and last 13 sts onto another needle.
Using long end left at toe, graft together sts from both needles to close toe.**

right sock

Using A, cast on 48 sts.
Distribute these sts evenly over 3 of the double-pointed needles and, using 4th needle, work in rounds as folls:
Rounds 1–15: *P2, k2, rep from * to end.
Break off A and join in B.
Round 16: K36, M1, k1, M1, k11. *50 sts*
Rounds 17–60: Knit.
Round 61: K11, k2tog, k1, k2togtbl, k34. *48 sts*
Rounds 62–70: Knit.
Round 71: K10, k2tog, k1, k2togtbl, k33. *46 sts*

Rounds 72–80: Knit.
Shape heel
Next round: Join in A and using A knit first 23 sts and turn, leaving rem 23 sts on holders.
Now working backwards and forwards in rows, not rounds, work on these 23 sts only for heel as folls:
Starting with a purl row and using A, work in st st for a further 9 rows, ending after a purl row.
Next row: K16, k2togtbl, turn.
Next row: P10, p2tog, turn.
Next row: K10, k2togtbl, turn.
Rep last 2 rows four more times, then first of these 2 rows again. *11 sts*
Break off A.
Shape foot
With RS facing, using B pick up and knit 6 sts up row-end edge of heel, knit 11 heel sts, pick up and knit 6 sts down other row-end edge of heel, then return to sts left on holders, knit these 23 sts. *46 sts*
Complete as given for Left Sock from ** to **.

TO MAKE UP
Weave in ends neatly, then press carefully.
Following chart, Swiss darn skull and crossed skis design onto outside of leg section, positioning row 1 of chart 43 rounds down from cast-on edge.

"Riding the mountain will be a joy in these beauties."

These Aran cuffed wellie socks are big enough at the top to be folded over your boots AND to tuck your jeans inside. I've used an organic yarn with a country feel that will wear very well and always look good. I love the muted natural colour for men.

Men's Aran wellie socks

Size
Approx 24cm from toe to heel

Yarn
Seven 50g balls of Garthenor 100% Organic Jacob in brown

Needles
Set of 4 double-pointed 6mm knitting needles

Other materials
Cable needle
Stitch holder
Knitter's sewing needle

Tension
20 rows and 15 stitches to 10cm square over st st using 6mm needles

Abbreviations
See page 109
C4B = slip next 2 stitches onto cable needle and leave at back of work, k2, then k2 from cable needle
MB = [k1, p1, k1, k1] all into next stitch, turn, p4, turn, k4, turn, [p2tog] twice, turn, k2tog

pattern (both alike)
Cast on 61 sts.
Distribute these sts evenly over 3 of the double-pointed needles and, using 4th needle, work in rounds as folls:
Round 1: P5, [k1, inc in next st, k1, p5] seven times. *68 sts*
Now work in cable and bobble patt as folls:
Round 2: P5, [C4B, p5] seven times.
Round 3: P5, [k5, p5] seven times.
Round 4: P2, MB, p2, [k4, p2, MB, p2] seven times.
Round 5: As round 3.
Rounds 2–5 form cable and bobble patt.
Cont in patt for a further 18 rounds.
Round 24: P5, *[k2tog] twice, p5, rep from * to end, wrap next st, turn (to reverse RS of work). *54 sts*
Rounds 25–29: Knit.
Round 30: K1, skpo, knit to last 3 sts, k2tog, k1. *52 sts*
Rep rounds 25–30 eight more times. *36 sts*
Rounds 79–82: Knit.

Shape heel
Now working backwards and forwards in rows, not rounds, shape heel as folls:
Row 1: K9, wrap next st, turn.
Row 2: P16, wrap next st, turn.
Row 3: K15, wrap next st, turn.
Row 4: P14, wrap next st, turn.
Row 5: K13, wrap next st, turn.
Row 6: P12, wrap next st, turn.
Row 7: K11, wrap next st, turn.
Row 8: P10, wrap next st, turn.
Row 9: K9, wrap next st, turn.
Row 10: P8, wrap next st, turn.
Row 11: K9, turn.
Row 12: P10, turn.
Row 13: K11, turn.
Row 14: P12, turn.
Row 15: K13, turn.
Row 16: P14, turn.
Row 17: K15, turn.
Row 18: P16, turn.
Row 19: K17, turn.
Row 20: P18.
Row 21: K9 but do NOT turn. (Heel completed.)
Now working in rounds again, distributing sts evenly over 3 needles, start to shape foot as folls:
Next round: Knit rem 9 sts of heel, knit 18 sts of top of foot, then knit first 9 heel sts. *36 sts*
Next round: Knit.
Rep last round until foot measures 20cm from back of heel.

Shape toe
Round 1: [K7, k2tog, skpo, k7] twice. *32 sts*
Round 2: Knit.
Round 3: [K6, k2tog, skpo, k6] twice. *28 sts*
Round 4: Knit.
Round 5: [K5, k2tog, skpo, k5] twice. *24 sts*
Round 6: Knit.
Round 7: [K4, k2tog, skpo, k4] twice. *20 sts*
Round 8: Knit.
Break yarn.
Slip first and last 5 sts onto one needle, and rem 10 sts onto another needle.
Graft together sts from both needles to close toe.

TO MAKE UP
Weave in ends neatly, then press carefully.

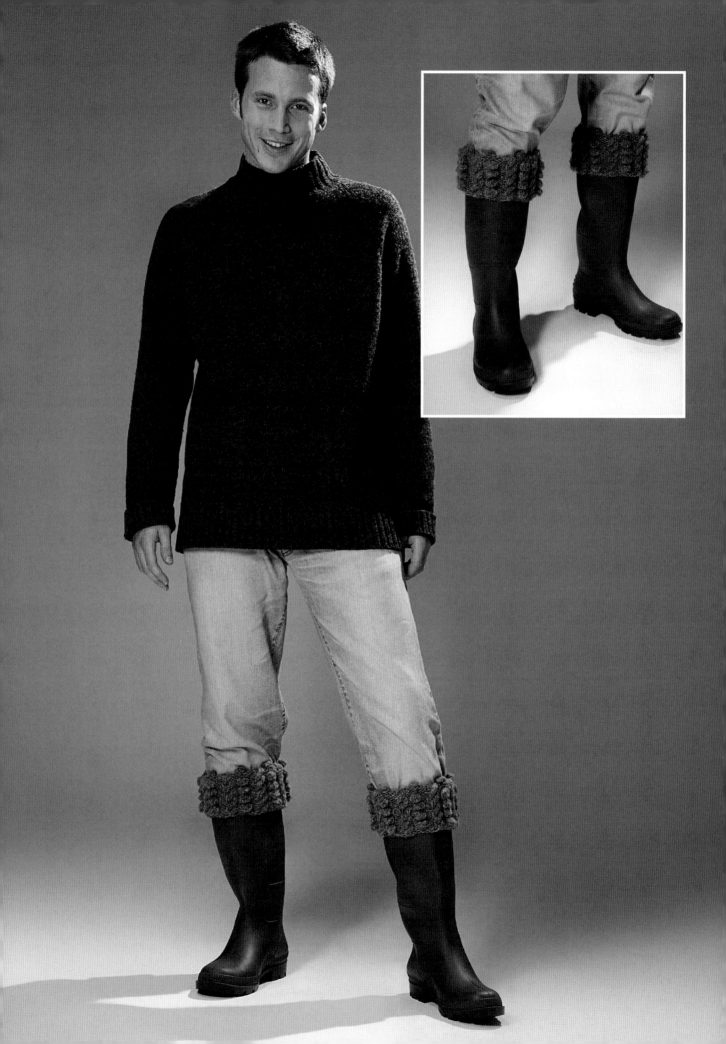

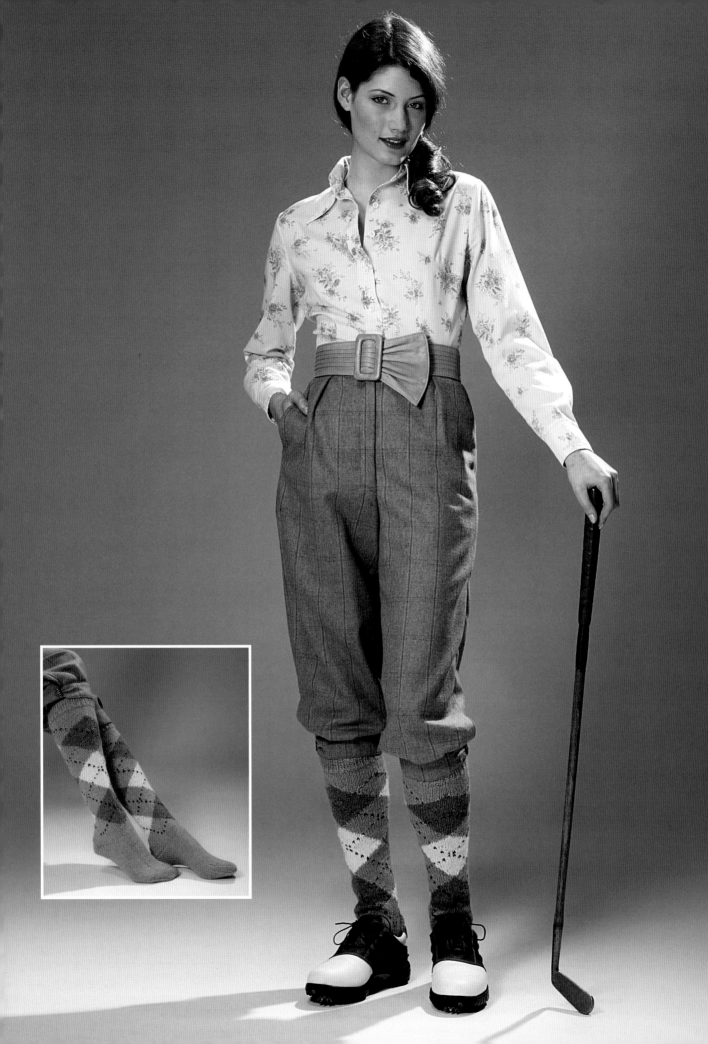

Argyle golf socks

pattern (both alike)

Using A, cast on 58 sts.

Row 1: *K1, p1, rep from * to end.

Rep the last row eleven more times.

Starting with a k row, work 8 rows st st.

Work 28 rows in patt from Chart. Rep Chart using C instead of B and B instead of C. Now work first 28 rows of Chart again.

Cont in A only.

Work a further 3cm, ending with a p row and dec 7 sts evenly across row.

51 sts

Cut yarn.

Change to double-pointed needles.

Shape heel

Slip next 13 sts on first needle, next 13 sts on second needle, next 13 sts on 3rd needle and last 12 sts on end of 1st needle.

Rejoin yarn to beg of first needle.

Next row: K24, turn.

Next row: Sl 1, p22, turn.

Next row: Sl 1, k21, turn.

Next row: Sl 1, p20, turn.

Cont in this way, working one less st on every row until the foll row has been worked:

Next row: Sl 1, p10, turn.

Next row: Sl 1, k11, turn.

Next row: Sl 1, p12, turn.

Cont in this way, working one more st on every row until the foll row has been worked:

Next row: Sl 1, p24, turn.

****Slip next 17 sts on first needle, next 17 sts on second needle and next 17 sts on 3rd needle.

Cont in rounds of st st until sock measures 14cm from **, decreasing one st at end of last round.

Shape toe

Next round: [K1, skpo, k19, K2tog, k1] twice.

Next round: K to end.

Next round: [K1, skpo, k17, K2tog, k1] twice.

Next round: K to end.

Next round: [K1, skpo, k15, K2tog, k1] twice.

Next round: K to end.

Cont in rounds decreasing on every alt round as set until the foll round has been worked:

Next round: [K1, skpo, k7, K2tog, k1] twice.

Slip first 11 sts onto one needle and rem 11 sts onto a second needle.

Fold sock inside out and cast one st from each needle off together.

TO MAKE UP

Weave in ends neatly, then press carefully. Join back leg seam.

All eyes will be turned your fair way if you knit your own Argyle golf socks. You'll be the envy of everyone on the green! Using brighter colours will give the socks a younger, fun feel.

Size
Approx 23cm from toe to heel

Yarn
Three 50g balls of RYC Baby Alpaca dk in fawn (A) and 1 ball each in cream (B), wine (C) and brown (D)

Needles
Pair of 4mm knitting needles
Set of 4 double-pointed 4mm knitting needles

Other materials
Knitter's sewing needle

Tension
30 rows and 24 sts to 10cm square over patt using 4mm needles

Abbreviations
See page 109

ARGYLE GOLF SOCKS

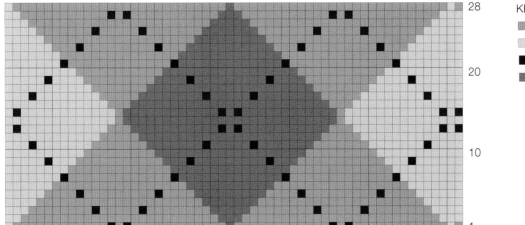

KEY
- A
- B
- C
- D

Even if you're not out on the playing field, these socks are an essential for avid football fans. What better way to support your team than by wearing their colours in the form of hand-knitted socks made with love.

Striped football socks

pattern (both alike)

Using A, cast on 54 sts.

Distribute these sts evenly over 3 of the double-pointed needles and, using 4th needle, work in rounds as folls:

Round 1: *K1, p1, rep from * to end.

Rep this round until sock measures 18cm from cast on edge.

Join in B.

Next round: Knit in B.

Rep last round fifteen more times.

Next round: Knit in A.

Rep last round fifteen more times.

Rep last 32 rounds once more.

Next round: Knit in B.

Next round: Using B, k5, [p1, k1] eight times, p1, k to end.

Rep last round fourteen more times.

Next round: Using A, k5, [p1, k1] eight times, p1, k to end.

Rep last round eight more times.

Next round: Knit in A.

Rep last round six more times.

Shape heel

Row 1: Using A, k26, turn.

Now working backwards and forwards in rows, not rounds, shape heel using A as folls:

Row 2: Sl 1, p24, turn.
Row 3: Sl 1, k23, turn.
Row 4: Sl 1, p22, turn.
Row 5: Sl 1, k21, turn.
Row 6: Sl 1, p20, turn.
Row 7: Sl 1, k19, turn.
Row 8: Sl 1, p18, turn.
Row 9: Sl 1, k17, turn.
Row 10: Sl 1, p16, turn.
Row 11: Sl 1, k15, turn.
Row 12: Sl 1, p14, turn.
Row 13: As row 11.
Row 14: As row 10.
Row 15: As row 9.
Row 16: As row 8.
Row 17: As row 7.
Row 18: As row 6.
Row 19: As row 5.
Row 20: As row 4.
Row 21: As row 3.
Row 22: As row 2.
Row 23: Sl 1, k25.
Row 24: Sl 1, p26.

Shape foot

Re-distribute all 54 sts over 3 of the 4 needles and now work in rounds as folls:

Next round: Knit in B.

Rep last round six more times.

Next round: Using B, k5, [p1, k1] eight times, p1, k to end.

Rep last round seventeen more times.

Next round: Knit in B.

Rep this round until sock measures 17cm from last heel row.

Shape toe

Break off B and complete toe using A.

Round 1: Knit.
Round 2: [Skpo, k23, k2tog] twice.
50 sts
Round 3: Knit.
Round 4: [Skpo, k21, k2tog] twice.
46 sts
Round 5: Knit.
Round 6: [Skpo, k19, k2tog] twice.
42 sts
Round 7: Knit.
Round 8: [Skpo, k17, k2tog] twice.
38 sts
Round 9: Knit.
Round 10: [Skpo, k15, k2tog] twice.
34 sts
Round 11: Knit.

Slip first 17 sts onto one needle and last 17 sts onto another needle. Join toe seam by grafting sts from both needles together.

TO MAKE UP

Weave in ends neatly, then press carefully.

Size
Approx 26.5cm from toe to heel

Yarn
Two 50g balls of Patons Diploma Gold DK in each of navy (A) and cream (B)

Needles
Set of 4 double-pointed 4mm knitting needles

Other materials
Stitch holder
Knitter's sewing needle

Tension
30 rows and 22 stitches to 10cm square over st st using 4mm needles

Abbreviations
See page 109

"An essential for avid football fans."

At home

Spotty slippers

pattern (both alike)

Using A, cast on 13 sts.

Distribute these sts evenly over 3 of the double-pointed needles and, using 4th needle, work in rounds as folls:

Round 1: Knit.

Round 2: [K2, M1] twice, k5, [M1, k2] twice. *17 sts*

Round 3: Knit.

Round 4: K3, M1, k2, M1, k7, M1, k2, M1, k3. *21 sts*

Round 5: Knit.

Round 6: K4, M1, k2, M1, k9, M1, k2, M1, k4. *25 sts*

Round 7: Knit.

Round 8: K5, M1, k2, M1, k11, M1, k2, M1, k5. *29 sts*

Round 9: Knit.

Round 10: K6, M1, k2, M1, k13, M1, k2, M1, k6. *33 sts*

Round 11: Knit.

Join in B.

Stranding yarn not in use loosely across WS of work, work in patt as folls:

Round 1: K2A, *k1B, k3A, rep from * to last 3 sts, k1B, k2A.

Rounds 2–4: Knit in A.

These 4 rounds form patt.

Work in patt for a further 12 rounds.

Now working backwards and forwards in rows, not rounds, cont as folls:

Next row: K2A, *k1B, k3A, rep from * to last 3 sts, k1B, k2A, turn.

Next row: Purl in A.

Next row: Knit in A.

Next row: Purl in A.

These 4 rows form patt for rest of slipper.

Work a further 14 rows, ending after a WS row.

Shape heel

Row 1: Patt 19 sts, sl 1, k2tog, psso, turn.

Row 2: Patt 6 sts, p3tog, turn.

Row 3: Patt 6 sts, sl 1, k2tog, psso, turn.

Rows 4–5: As rows 2–3.

Row 6: As row 2.

Row 7: Patt 6 sts, skpo, turn.

Row 8: Patt 6 sts, p2tog, turn.

Rep last 2 rows six more times.

Cast off rem 7 sts.

TO MAKE UP

Weave in ends neatly, then press carefully. Join toe seam. Make four 3-cm diameter pom-poms using A and B and sew two pom-poms to heel of each slipper as in photograph.

With their very girlie and modern feel, these slippers are my favourites. I love the pink and white but they'll also look great in black with white spots and in all manner of unusual colour options. Using thick yarn makes them ideal for winter.

Size
Approx 23cm from toe to heel

Yarn
Two 50g balls of Rowan Little Big Wool in pink (A) and one ball in white (B)

Needles
Set of 4 double-pointed 8mm knitting needles

Other materials
Knitter's sewing needle

Tension
20 rows and 16 stitches to 10cm square over patt using 8mm needles

Abbreviations
See page 109

"These slippers have a very girlie and modern feel."

I love these little socks, which are another cool thing I've found on my travels. They are great for hanging off bags and belt loops, using as keyrings, hanging from your car mirror and practically anywhere else that needs a bit of brightening up. Use bold colours and give them to all your friends as gifts.

Turkish mini socks

pattern (both alike)

Using A, cast on 4 sts.
Distribute these sts evenly over 3 of the double-pointed needles and, using 4th needle, work in rounds as folls:

Round 1: Inc once in each st to end. *8 sts*

Round 2: K1, [M1, k2] three times, M1, k1. *12 sts*

Round 3: [K1, M1, k4, M1, k1] twice. *16 sts*

Joining in and breaking off yarns as required and stranding yarn not in use loosely across WS of work, now work in patt from chart as folls:

Work 8 rounds.

Shape heel

Next round: Using A, k15, wrap next st, turn.

Now working backwards and forwards in rows using A, complete heel as folls:

Next row: P4, wrap next st, turn.

Next row: K3, wrap next st, turn.

Next row: P2, wrap next st, turn.

Next row: K3, turn.

Next row: P4, turn.

Next row: K5.

Distribute all 16 sts over 3 of the double pointed needles and, using 4th needle, now start to work in rounds again as folls:

Starting with chart row 10, work following chart for a further 14 rounds, thereby completing all 23 rows of chart. Cast off.

TO MAKE UP

Sew toe seam.

Using A and 2.50mm crochet hook, attach yarn to cast off edge and work around cast off edge, working into cast off sts, as folls: 1 ss into first st, * (1 ss, 3 ch, ss to 3rd ch from hook) into next st, 1 ss into each of next 2 sts, rep from * to end.

Fasten off.

Fold sock flat, with heel at back.

Using C and 2.50mm crochet hook, starting and ending level with first round worked using C, work 1 row of ss around entire foot section as in photograph.

Fasten off.

Using A and C together, make 2 twisted cords, each approx 15cm long, and knot one end of each, leaving a small tassel of about 1.5cm. Attach other end of each cord to inside of top edge of sock.

Weave in ends neatly, then press carefully.

Size
Approx 7.5cm from top to toe

Yarn
Small amounts of 4-ply yarn in red (A), bottle green or denim blue (B) and cream or pale blue (C)

Needles
Set of 4 double-pointed 3.25mm knitting needles
2.50mm crochet hook

Other materials
Stitch holders
Knitter's sewing needle

Tension
36 rows and 28 stitches to 10cm square over patt using 3.25mm needles

Abbreviations
See page 109
ch = chain
ss = slip stitch

TURKISH MINI SOCKS

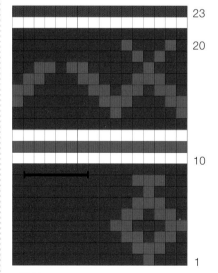

KEY
■ A
■ B
□ C

—— Heel placement

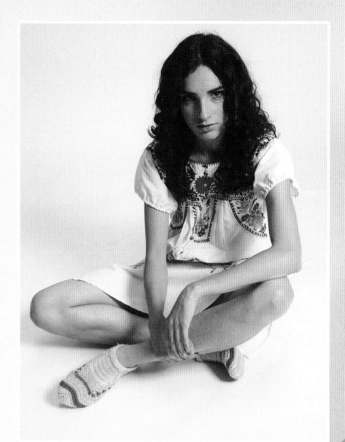

> **"A bit of extra warmth on chilly nights at home."**

TV slippers

pattern (both alike)

Using A, cast on 94 sts.

Work in garter stitch for 4 rows, inc 1 st at each end of 2nd and foll 2 rows and ending after a WS row. *100 sts*

Join in B.

Using B, work in garter stitch for 4 rows.

Join in C.

Using C, work in garter stitch for 4 rows.

Using A, work in garter stitch for 4 rows, ending after a WS row.

Shape upper

Row 1: Using B, k2, [sl 1, k3] ten times, sl 1, k2togtbl, k10, k2tog, sl 1, [k3, sl 1] ten times, k2. *98 sts*

Row 2: Using B, k2, [sl 1, k3] ten times, k2tog, p10, k2togtbl, [k3, sl 1] ten times, k2. *96 sts*

Row 3: Using A, k4, [sl 1, k3] nine times, sl 1, k2togtbl, k10, k2tog, sl 1, [k3, sl 1] nine times, k4. *94 sts*

Row 4: Using A, k4, [sl 1, k3] nine times, k2tog, p10, k2togtbl, [k3, sl 1] nine times, k4. *92 sts*

These 4 rows set the sts – central 10 sts in st st with sts either side in textured patt.

Place markers either side of centre 10 sts.

Keeping sts correct as set, cont as folls:

Row 5: Using C, patt to within 2 sts of first marker, k2togtbl, slip marker onto right needle, k10, slip second marker onto right needle, k2tog, patt to end.

Row 6: Using C, patt to within 2 sts of first marker, k2tog, slip marker onto right needle, p10, slip second marker onto right needle, k2togtbl, patt to end.

Break off C.

Using B, rep rows 5–6.

Using A, rep rows 5–6.

Rep last 4 rows three more times, then first 3 of these rows again. *52 sts*

Next row: Using A, k2tog, patt to marker, slip marker onto right needle, p10, slip second marker onto right needle, patt to last 2 sts, k2tog. *50 sts*

Using B, patt 2 rows.

Using A, patt 2 rows.

Rep last 4 rows once more, ending after a WS row.

Break off A.

Using B, work in garter stitch for 5 rows, ending after a RS row.

Cast off knitwise (on WS).

TO MAKE UP

Weave in ends neatly, then press carefully. Join sole and heel seam.

These comfy, textural slipper socks are an unusual but practical shape. As they come up high enough to cover your ankles they will give you that extra bit of warmth on chilly nights at home watching TV.

Size
Approx 23cm from toe to heel

Yarn
One 50g ball of Rowan Pure Wool DK in each of pale green (A), shaded blue/cream/lavender (B) and denim blue (C)

Needles
Pair of 3.75mm knitting needles

Other materials
Knitter's sewing needle

Tension
40 rows and 22 stitches to 10cm square over garter stitch using 3.75mm needles

Abbreviations
See page 109

Note
When working textured patt, slip all sts purlwise with yarn at WS of work – this is back on RS rows, or front on WS rows

Slouch socks

Note: To make the tucks, fold the previous rounds up inside the work and catch the top back loop of the stitch on the stated round in with the stitch of this round. Don't worry too much if you don't pick up exactly the right st, or the right round – this will add to the slouchy look!

pattern (both alike)

Cast on 46 sts.

Distribute these sts evenly over 3 of the double-pointed needles and, using 4th needle, work in rounds as folls:

Round 1: *K1, p1, rep from * to end.

Rounds 2–14: Knit.

Make first tuck

Round 15: K9, [knit next st tog with corresponding st 10 rounds below] twenty times, k17.

Rounds 16–24: Knit.

Make second tuck

Round 25: K2, [knit next st tog with corresponding st 5 rounds below] ten times, k34.

Rounds 26–34: Knit.

Make third tuck

Round 35: K23, [knit next st tog with corresponding st 12 rounds below] twenty-two times, k1.

Rounds 36–40: Knit.

Round 41: K11, k2tog, k2togtbl, k31. *44 sts*

Rounds 42–49: Knit.

Make fourth tuck

Round 50: K4, [knit next st tog with corresponding st 7 rounds below] eighteen times, k22.

Round 51: K10, k2tog, k2togtbl, k30. *42 sts*

Rounds 52–60: Knit.

Round 61: K9, k2tog, k2togtbl, k29. *40 sts*

Rounds 62–63: Knit.

Make fifth tuck

Round 64: K23, [knit next st tog with corresponding st 9 rounds below]

twelve times, k5.

Rounds 65–67: Knit.

Make sixth tuck

Round 68: K3, [knit next st tog with corresponding st 5 rounds below] ten times, k27.

Rounds 69–70: Knit.

Shape heel

Left sock only

Row 1: K19, wrap next st, turn.

Right sock only

Row 1: K39, wrap next st, turn.

Both socks

Now working backwards and forwards in rows, not rounds, shape heel as folls:

Row 2: P18, wrap next st, turn.

Row 3: K17, wrap next st, turn.

Row 4: P16, wrap next st, turn.

Row 5: K15, wrap next st, turn.

Row 6: P14, wrap next st, turn.

Row 7: K13, wrap next st, turn.

Row 8: P12, wrap next st, turn.

Row 9: K11, wrap next st, turn.

Row 10: P10, wrap next st, turn.

Row 11: K11, turn.

Row 12: P12, turn.

Row 13: K13, turn.

Row 14: P14, turn.

Row 15: K15, turn.

Row 16: P16, turn.

Row 17: K17, turn.

Row 18: P18, turn.

Row 19: K19, turn.

Row 20: P20, turn.

Row 21: Knit to end of round.

Redistribute all 40 sts over 3 of the 4 needles. (Heel complete.)

Next round: Knit to end.

Rep last round thirty-two more times.

Shape toe

Round 1: [K2togtbl, k16, k2tog] twice. *36 sts*

Round 2: Knit.

Round 3: [K2togtbl, k14, k2tog] twice. *32 sts*

Round 4: Knit.

Size
Approx 21cm from toe to heel

Yarn
Two 50g balls of Rowan Kid Classic in aubergine

Needles
Set of 4 double-pointed 5mm knitting needles

Other materials
Stitch holder
Knitter's sewing needle

Tension
25 rows and 19 stitches to 10cm square over st st using 5mm needles

Abbreviations
See page 109

Round 5: [K2togtbl, k12, k2tog] twice. *28 sts*

Round 6: Knit.

Round 7: [K2togtbl, k10, k2tog] twice. *24 sts*

Round 8: Knit.

Break yarn, leaving a long end.

Slip first 12 sts onto one needle, and last 12 sts onto another needle.

Using long end left at toe, graft together sts from both needles to close toe.

TO MAKE UP

Weave in ends neatly.

Cherry slippers

What cuties!
Form fitting
slippers are
great for lazing
around the house
without dragging
your heels and
you can easily
slip a pair of
shoes on top if
you need to dash
outside. I love
the cherry
design and think
they would also
work beautifully
with a cream
background
instead of black.

pattern (both alike)

Using A, cast on 18 sts.

Distribute these sts evenly over 3 of the double-pointed needles and, using 4th needle, work in rounds as folls:

Round 1: Knit.

Place markers on needles at beg of round and after first/last 9 sts.

Round 2: [M1, k to marker, slip marker onto right needle] twice.

Round 3: [K to marker, M1, slip marker onto right needle] twice. *22 sts*

Rounds 4–10: Rep rounds 2–3 three more times then rep round 2 again. *36 sts*

Keeping increases as now set (by inc 2 sts on every round and alternating which side of markers these incs are worked), now work in patt from chart A as folls:

Work 1 round. *38 sts*

Joining in and breaking off yarns as required and stranding yarn not in use loosely across WS of work, work rounds 2–16. *68 sts* (All increases completed.)

Cont straight until chart round 45 has been completed.

Shape for sole

Next round: Using B, k10, cast off next 48 sts loosely, k to end of round, then k first 10 sts again, turn.

Now working backwards and forwards in rows, not rounds, cont on these 20 sts only as folls:

Starting with a WS row, work all 16 rows of chart B twice, then first 8 rows again, ending after a RS row.

Break off B and cont using A only.

Shape heel

Dec 1 st at each end of next 5 rows, ending after a WS row.

Break yarn and leave rem 10 sts on a holder.

Shape back and side section

With RS facing and using A, starting at cast off edge at base of sole section, pick up and knit 36 sts up row-end edge of sole to sts left on holder at heel, k these 10 heel sts inc 1 st at centre, then pick up and knit 36 sts down other row-end edge of sole sts. *83 sts*

Working backwards and forwards in rows, not rounds, cont as folls:

Work 5 rows, ending after a WS row.

Now work all 14 rows of chart C.

Using A, work 2 rows, ending after a WS row.

Cast off loosely.

TO MAKE UP

Weave in ends neatly, then press carefully. Join toe seam. Sew row-end edges of back and side section to cast off edge of section worked in rounds, leaving approx 4cm free on top of foot.

Edging

With RS facing and using 3.00mm crochet hook, attach A to cast off edge of back and side section at back of heel, make 5 ch, then, spacing sts evenly, work around opening edge of slipper as folls: *1 tr into edge, 2 ch, rep from * to end, ss to 3rd of 5 ch at beg of round.

Fasten off.

Using photograph as a guide, oversew through holes of crochet edging using B double and tie ends in a bow.

Size
Approx 23cm from toe to heel

Yarn
One 50g ball of Rowan 4-ply Soft in each of black (A), red (B), white (C) and green (D)

Needles
Set of 4 double-pointed 3mm knitting needles
3.00mm crochet hook

Other materials
Stitch holder
Knitter's sewing needle

Tension
45 rows and 35 stitches to 10cm square over patt using 3mm needles

Abbreviations
See page 109
ch = chain
tr = treble
ss = slip stitch

CHERRY SLIPPERS

Chart A

Chart B

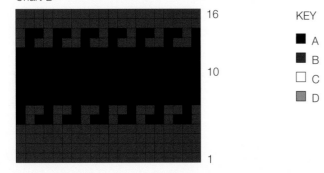

KEY

■ A
■ B
□ C
■ D

Chart C

"**What cuties! I love the cherry design.** "

Christmas stocking

pattern

Using A, cast on 68 sts.

Starting with a k row, work 46 rows in st st.

Change to B.

Work in st st until sock measures 30cm, ending after a purl row.

Shape upper foot

Inc row: K30, M1, k8, M1, k30.

Work 3 rows st st.

Inc row: K30, M1, k10, M1, k30.

Work 3 rows st st.

Inc row: K30, M1, k12, M1, k30.

Work 3 rows st st.

Cont in this way, inc 2 sts on next and every 4th row until there are 88 sts.

Purl 1 row.

Divide for foot

Next row: Cast off one st, k next 5 sts, leave these 6 sts on a holder, cast off next 26 sts, k next 21 sts, cast off next 26 sts, k rem 6 sts, leave these 7 sts on a holder.

Break yarn.

With WS facing, return to centre 22 sts, rejoin B, p to end.

Cont in st st for a further 4cm.

Mark each end of last row with a coloured thread.

Work a further 4 rows.

Shape toe

Next row: K2, skpo, k to last 4 sts, k2tog, k2.

Next row: Purl to end.

Rep the last 2 rows five more times.

10 sts

Leave these sts on a holder.

Heel

With WS facing, return to 6 sts on first holder, join on B at inner edge, p6, then, working across sts on second holder, cast off first st, p to end. *12 sts*

Work 8 rows st st.

Break yarn.

Sole

With RS facing and B, pick up and k8 sts up right side of heel, skpo, k8, k2tog across heel sts, pick up and k8 sts down left side of heel. *26 sts*

Starting with a p row, cont in st st until sole fits along cast off edge and row ends to coloured threads.

Shape toe

Next row: K2, skpo, k to last 4 sts, k2tog, k2.

Next row: P to end.

Rep the last 2 rows seven more times. *10 sts*

Leaving a long end break off yarn, thread through sts of sole and upper foot, draw up tightly and secure.

TO MAKE UP

Reversing seam on first 8cm, join back seam to heel. Join sole to upper from heel to toe.

Using A and following photograph, embroider Christmas tree and stars. Fold cuff to right side. Attach sequins. Attach ribbon to back seam to make hanging loop.

This Christmas stocking is big enough to keep St Nick busy leading up to the festive season. It can be customised for everyone in the family by embroidering a name or making funny festive faces with sequins, yarn, beads, trims and ribbons.

Size
Approx 26cm from toe to heel and 38cm long with cuff turned over

Yarn
One 50g ball of Rowan Pure Wool DK in white (A) and two balls in red (B)

Needles
Pair of 4mm knitting needles

Other materials
Stitch holders
Knitter's sewing needle
20cm of ribbon
12 sequins
Sewing needle and thread

Tension
30 rows and 22 sts to 10cm square over st st using 4mm needles

Abbreviations
See page 109

"A stocking big enough to keep St Nick busy."

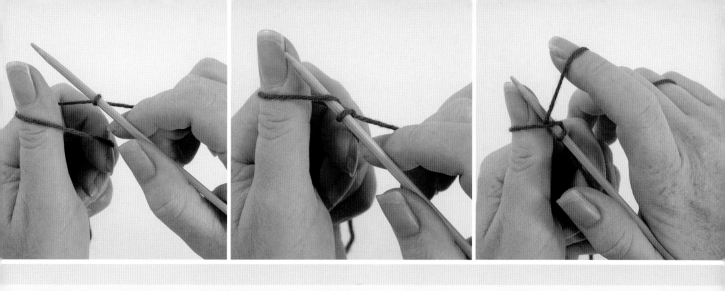

Equipment and techniques

knitting equipment

You don't need much equipment to start knitting: here are some essentials and some useful pieces.

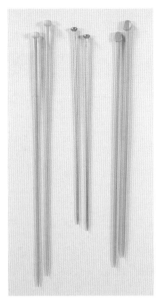

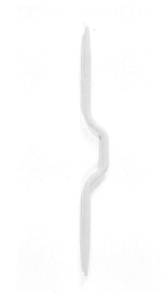

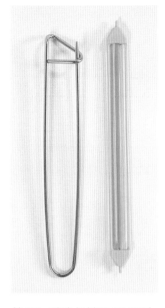

Above: knitting needles come in various sizes and materials; left to right, bamboo, metal and plastic. Each pattern gives the size of needle you need, but the material is up to you. Novice knitters may find bamboo needles easiest to use as the yarn does not slip so easily on them, making dropping a stitch less likely.

Above: double-pointed knitting needles have, as the name suggests, a point at each end. This allows you to knit from either end and so knit in the round. They, too, are available in different materials.

Above: the cable needle shown is a cranked one, which holds the stitches securely while you work the cable, but you can also buy straight cable needles, which are quicker to use.

Above: stitch holders are used to keep some stitches safe while you work on another part of the project. They usually look like giant safety pins (left), but the double-ended type (right) are useful as you can knit straight off either end of them, rather than having to put the stitches back on a knitting needle first.

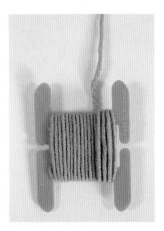

Left: when you are working colour knitting, wind lengths of the yarns you are using onto separate bobbins and knit from these to avoid ending up with a horrible tangle of balls of yarn.

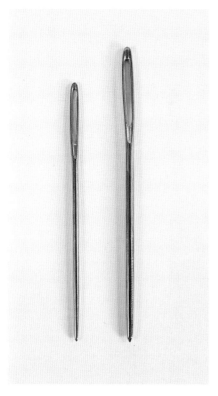

Above: knitter's sewing needles have a blunt point to help prevent them splitting the yarn when you are sewing up a project.

Above: use a solid ruler, either a metal or a plastic one, to measure your tension (see page 108).

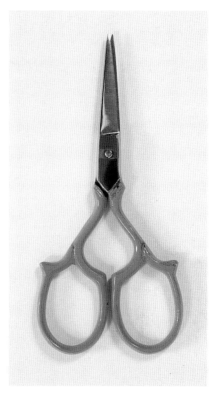

Above: keep a pair of small, sharp scissors to hand for cutting yarn. Don't try and break yarn with your hands, some types are surprisingly strong.

Above: there are various types of round marker, from metal rings to the pretty, beaded type shown. Alternatively, you can just use a loop of contrast-colour yarn.

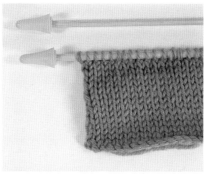

Above: point protectors are not essential, but they are useful. They stop the stitches falling off your needle when you are not knitting, and they stop the points of your needles punching holes in your knitting bag.

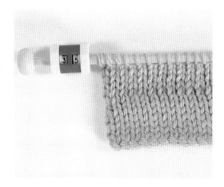

Above: a row counter is another non-essential item that you might find useful. Put it on a knitting needle and clock up each row as you work it, then you will never loose your place in a pattern.

tension

When you buy a pattern it will specify the yarn you should use to knit it and the tension the pattern requires. This is the number of stitches and rows to a specific measurement, usually 10cm. It is important that you work to the tension the pattern asks for or the finished item will be too big (if your tension is too loose), or too small (if your tension is too tight). So, even though you are desperate to start your project, take an hour or so to knit a swatch and measure it carefully. In the long run this takes much less time (and prevents a lot of disappointment) than knitting the whole project and finding that it doesn't fit.

knitting a tension swatch

First, find the tension information in the pattern. It will say something like: '22 stitches and 28 rows to 10cm square over stocking stitch using 4mm needles'. What this means it that, using the right sort of yarn and needles and working the right stitch pattern, in a piece of knitting measuring 10cm by 10cm you must have 22 stitches in one direction and 28 rows in the other direction.

So, use the yarn and needles specified in the pattern to cast on the number of stitches stated, plus ten. Knit the number of rows stated – in the stitch pattern specified – plus ten, then cast off. Make the cast off as loose as you can to avoid pulling in the top edge of the knitting.

measuring stitches   measuring rows

measuring your tension

The next step is to measure your tension. Do this carefully, or knitting the swatch will have been a waste of your time. It is important to measure a few stitches or rows in from the edges as the cast on and cast off edges and the row ends can be tighter or looser than the stitches in the middle of the knitting, which are the ones that matter here.

Lay the swatch flat, without stretching it at all. To count the number of stitches, lay a ruler across the swatch so that 10cm (or the distance stated in the pattern) is measured out a few stitches in from either edge. Put a knitter's pin into the swatch at either end of the measured distance. Remove the ruler and count the number of stitches between the pins.

To count the number of rows, repeat the process, but lay the ruler vertically on the swatch so that 10cm is measured out a few rows from either edge.

altering your tension

If you have the same numbers of stitches and rows as stated in the pattern, then you have the correct tension. You can go ahead and knit the project your fingers have been itching to do.

However, if you do not have the right numbers of stitches and rows, you need to alter your tension. Do not do this by trying to knit more tightly or loosely. Everyone has a 'natural' tension, the tension they naturally knit to, and if you try to knit to a different tension your stitches will just be uneven. Also, you will usually forget that you are trying to knit more tightly and your natural tension will reassert itself, then you are back to square one.

The way to alter your tension is to change the size of the knitting needles you are using. If you have too few stitches and rows, knit the swatch again using needles one size smaller. So, if the pattern asks for 5mm needles, try again using 4.5mm needles.

If you have too many stitches and rows, then try again with needles one size larger: 5.5mm needles instead of 5mm.

This may sound time-consuming and annoying, but, as I said before, it's much better to knit a little square a few times than to spend more time and effort knitting a whole project that doesn't fit.

abbreviations

Here is a list of the abbreviations you will find in the knitting patterns in this book.

A, B, C, etc	colours as indicated in the pattern
alt	alternate
approx	approximate
beg	begin, beginning, begins
C4B	cable four (or number stated) back
C4F	cable four (or number stated) forward
cm	centimetre(s)
cont	continue
dec(s)	decrease, decreasing, decreases
DK	double knitting
dpn	double-pointed needle(s)
foll(s)	following, follows
g	gram(s)
inc(s)	increase, increasing, increases
incl	including
k2tog	knit two together
k	knit
m	metre(s)
mm	millimetres
M1	make one stitch
p2tog	purl two together
p	purl
patt(s)	pattern(s)
psso	pass slipped stitch over
rem	remain, remaining
rep(s)	repeat(s)
rev st st	reverse stocking stitch
RS	right side
skpo	slip one, knit one, pass slipped stitch over
sl	slip
st(s)	stitch(es)
st st	stocking stitch
tbl	through the back loop
tog	together
WS	wrong side
yo	yarn over
*	repeat instructions between/following * as many times as instructed
[]	repeat instructions between [ ] as many times as instructed

needle sizes

Knitting needles are sold in standard sizes, though there are three different measuring systems. This chart compares sizes across all three systems.

US	metric	old UK and Canadian
50	25	–
35	19	–
19	15	–
15	10	000
13	9	00
11	8	0
11	7.5	1
10½	7	2
10½	6.5	3
10	6	4
9	5.5	5
8	5	6
7	4.5	7
6	4	8
5	3.75	9
4	3.5	–
3	3.25	10
⅔	3	11
2	2.75	12
1	2.25	13
0	2	14

weights and lengths

If you need to convert the weights or lengths given in this book, then use the chart below. Whichever system of measurement you use, metric or imperial, do stick with it throughout a project, as changing systems midway can lead to trouble.

oz = g x 0.0352
g = oz x 28.57
in = cm x 0.3937
cm = in x 2.54
yd = m x 1.0936
m = yd x 0.9144

knitting techniques

Practice any unfamiliar techniques on scrap yarn before embarking on your knitted project.

holding yarn and needles

There is no right or wrong way of holding the yarn and needles, so try these popular methods and use whichever feels most comfortable.

In the UK and USA the usual way is to hold the left-hand needle from above, rather like a knife, and the right-hand needle in the crook of your thumb, rather like a pen. The working end of the yarn goes over the right index finger, under the second finger and over the ring finger to help control the tension of the stitches. The right index finger moves back and forth to wind the yarn around the tip of the right-hand needle.

The other method, often called the 'continental method', also holds the right-hand needle like a pen, but the left-hand needle is held between the thumb and second finger. The working yarn goes over the left index finger, under the second and ring fingers and over the little finger to control the tension. The left index finger is held aloft and moves back and forth to wind the yarn around the tip of the right-hand needle.

The same principles apply when knitting in the round on four needles. Bring the lower end of the needle holding the stitches being worked over the top of the end of the needle below to it to allow you to knit easily. You can safely ignore the two other needles holding stitches: as long as the stitches are not too close to either end of the needle, they won't fall off.

slip knot

The starting point for any piece of knitting is a slip knot. There is more than one way of making this, but the result is the same.

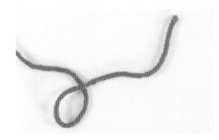

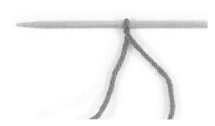

1 Lay the tail end of the yarn over the ball end to form a loop.

2 Bring the tail end under the loop of yarn. Slip the tip of a knitting needle under this tail end, as shown.

3 Pull on both ends of the yarn and the slip knot will tighten around the needle. This will always be your first cast on stitch.

After you have knitted the first couple of rows, you can pull gently on the tail end of the yarn to tighten the first stitch if it is a little bit baggy.

thumb cast on

This cast on has an elastic edge that matches in well with the look of garter, rib and moss stitch (see page 115), so if you are casting on for the rib of a pair of socks, this is the method to use. When casting on onto double-pointed needles, you can put a point protector on one end if you are worried about the stitches falling off. If you are working in double-knitting yarn, making a slip knot about 50cm from the end will allow you to cast on about 40 stitches.

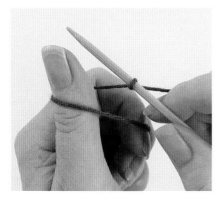

1 Make a slip knot about the necessary distance from the end of the yarn. Hold the needle with the knot on in your right hand. *Wind the tail end of the yarn clockwise around your left thumb.

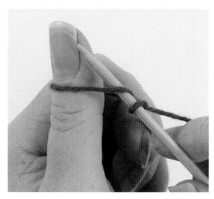

2 Put the tip of the needle under the loop of yarn around your thumb.

3 With your right index finger, wind the ball end of the yarn around the tip of the needle, taking it between the needle and your thumb and then around to the front.

4 Bring the knitting needle, and the ball end loop around it, through the loop on your thumb.

5 Slip the loop off your thumb. Pull gently on the tail end of the yarn to tighten the stitch.

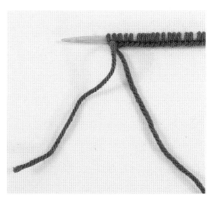

6 Repeat from * until you have cast the number of stitches needed onto the needle.

cable cast on

This method of casting on produces a neat, firm edge that matches in perfectly with the look of stocking stitch. Use this method to cast on for the toe of a sock or within a pattern. Always make the slip knot about 15cm from the end of the yarn to leave enough to weave in the end later.

1 Hold the needle with the knot on in your left hand. From left to right, put the tip of the right-hand needle into the front of the knot.

2 *Wind the ball end of the yarn around the tip of the right-hand needle, going under and then over the top of the needle.

3 Bring the right-hand knitting needle, and the loop of yarn around the tip of it, through the slip knot.

4 Slip the loop of yarn on the right-hand needle onto the left-hand needle and pull gently on the ball end of the yarn to tighten the stitch. You have cast on a second stitch.

5 For all the following stitches, put the right-hand needle between the two previous stitches, instead of through the last stitch.

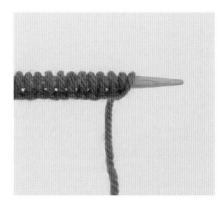

6 Repeat from * until you have cast the number of stitches needed onto the needle.

knit stitch

This is the first and most basic stitch you need to learn to start knitting, and it is very similar to the cable cast on (see page 112). First cast on the number of stitches needed for the project, using whichever cast on method is most appropriate.

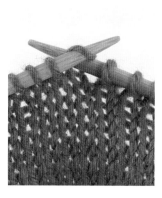   

1 *From left to right, put the tip of the right-hand needle into the front of the next stitch on the left-hand needle.

2 Wind the working yarn around the tip of the right-hand needle, going under and then over the top of the needle.

3 Bring the right-hand needle, and the loop of yarn around it, through the stitch on the left-hand needle.

4 Keeping the loop on the right-hand needle, slip the original stitch off the left-hand needle. You have knitted a stitch. Repeat from * until you have knitted all the stitches on the left-hand needle. Then swap the needles in your hands and you are ready to begin the next row.

purl stitch

This is the other basic stitch used in knitting.

1 *From right to left, put the tip of the right-hand needle into the front of the next stitch on the left-hand needle.

2 From front to back, wind the working yarn over the tip of the right-hand needle.

3 Bring the right-hand needle, and the loop of yarn around it, through the stitch on the left-hand needle.

4 Keeping the loop on the right-hand needle, slip the original stitch off the left-hand needle. You have purled a stitch. Repeat from * until you have purled all the stitches on the left-hand needle. Then swap the needles in your hands and you are ready to begin the next row.

casting off

This is the way you finish off your knitting, securing the stitches so that they don't unravel. It is shown here on a knit row, but can be worked just as well on a purl row: simply purl the stitches instead of knitting them.

1 Knit the first two stitches on the left-hand needle.

2 *Put the tip of the left-hand needle into the first stitch you knitted and lift it over the second stitch. Drop this first stitch off both needles.

3 Knit another stitch and repeat from * to cast off all the stitches in turn.

4 When you have just one stitch left on the right-hand needle, pull gently to open it up a little and slip it off the needle. Cut the yarn 15cm from the knitting. Thread the cut end through the last stitch and pull gently on the cut end to tighten the stitch.

knitting in the round

This is the technique used to work seamless tubes of knitting for making socks. It might seem fiddly at first, but do persevere as it isn't actually difficult once you get the hang of manipulating the four needles. An advantage of working in the round is that you only have to knit stitches – no purl rows – to make stocking stitch. You can more or less ignore the needles that you are not actually knitting with.

1 Cast on the correct number of stitches using the appropriate cast on method (see pages 111–112) and double-pointed needles. To distribute the stitches evenly between the needles, just slip one-third of them off one end of the needle onto a second needle. Slip another third of them off the other end of the needle onto a third needle. If you push the stitches to the middle of the needle they should just hang there without falling off.

2 Before you join the stitches into the round, slip a stitch marker onto the free end of one needle. Make sure that the row of stitches is lying in a straight line across the three needles; not twisted at all. Now, put the fourth needle in the set through the first stitch you cast on. Wrap the working end of the yarn firmly around the tip of the fourth needle and knit the stitch, pulling it tight so that the three needles with stitches on form a triangle.

3 Continue knitting the stitches on the first needle. When they are all knitted, then that needle is freed up to become the spare needle for working the stitches on the next needle.

4 Just keep knitting the stitches off each needle in turn to create a knitted tube. When you reach the stitch marker, slip it onto the next needle so that you always know where the beginning of the round is. Knit the first stitch on each needle firmly, pulling the yarn tight, to prevent gaps appearing in the knitting where the needles 'join'. If they do appear, then occasionally knit one stitch off the next needle for a round to change the position of the 'joins'.

knitted fabrics

Now that you can knit, you can create knitted fabrics with different stitch patterns. Shown here are swatches of the four most popular simple knitted fabrics.

garter stitch
This is the most basic knitted fabric as it is with knit stitches only.

To work garter stitch cast on as many stitches as you need.
Knit every row.

stocking stitch (st st)
This is the most popular knitted fabric and made by working alternate rows of knit and purl stitches. The other side of this fabric is called reverse stocking stitch (rev st st).

To work stocking stitch, cast on as many stitches as you need.
Row 1: Knit.
Row 2: Purl.
Repeat rows 1–2. It's not really any more difficult than garter stitch. If you get confused as to whether you should be knitting or purling on the next row, just hold the needle with the stitches on in your left hand and look at the side facing you. If that is the right side, as shown above, then the next row will be a knit row. If the wrong side is facing you, the next row will be a purl row.

rib stitch
This is usually used to make cuffs and collars as it is very stretchy. There are various types of rib stitch: shown here is single rib (1 x 1 rib).

To work single rib stitch cast on an odd number of stitches.
Row 1: [K1, p1] rep to last st, k1.
Row 2: [P1, k1] rep to last st, p1.
Repeat rows 1–2.
After you have knitted the first stitch, bring the yarn between the tips of the needles to the front of the work ready to purl the next stitch. When you have purled, take the yarn to the back again to knit the next stitch.

moss stitch
This is a decorative stitch that makes a flat, firm border on garments and accessories.

To work moss stitch cast on an odd number of stitches.
Row 1: [K1, p1] rep to last st, k1.
Repeat row 1.
Bring the yarn forward to purl and take it back again to knit in the same way as for rib stitch. If you get confused as to which stitch you should be working next, look at the previous one. If it has a bump across it then it is a purl stitch and the next stitch will be knit. If the last stitch is smooth, then you knitted it and the next stitch will be purl.

increases

Increasing is making extra stitches in a row to make the knitting wider or to shape it. There are various different ways of doing this, but shown here are the most commonly used methods.

increase (inc)
This method involves knitting twice into a stitch. The increase is visible in the finished knitting as the second stitch made has a small bar of yarn across the bottom of it.

1 Knit to the position of the increase. Knit into the next stitch in the usual way (see page 113), but do not drop the original stitch off the left-hand needle.

2 Now knit into the back of the same stitch on the left-hand needle, then drop it off the needle.
 You have made two stitches out of one and so increased by one stitch.

make one (M1)
This method involves creating a brand new stitch between two existing ones, It is almost completely invisible in the finished knitting.

1 Knit to the position of the increase. Using the tip of the left-hand needle, pick up the loop of yarn lying between the next two stitches. Pick it up by putting the tip of the needle through the front of the loop.

2 Knit into the back of the picked-up loop on the left-hand needle, then drop the loop.
 You have created a completely new stitch and so increased by one stitch.

decreases

Decreasing involves taking away stitches in a row to make the knitting narrower. Again, there are various different ways of doing this, but shown here are the two most popular methods. These decreases slant in different directions, so when used at either end of a row, they mirror each other.

knit two together (k2tog) In this
method you knit two stitches together to make one. The decrease slants to the right on a knit row.

purl two together (p2tog) This
uses the same principle as k2tog to decrease stitches on a purl row. The decrease slants to the left on a purl row.

 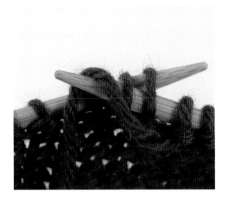

Knit to the position of the decrease. From left to right, put the tip of the right-hand needle through the front of the second stitch from the end of the left-hand needle, then through the first one. Knit the two stitches together in the usual way, just as if they were one.

You have made two stitches into one and so decreased by one stitch.

Purl to the position of the decrease. From right to left, put the tip of the right-hand needle through the next two stitches on the left-hand needle. Purl the two stitches together in the usual way, just as if they were one.

You have made two stitches into one and so decreased by one stitch.

slip one, knit one pass slipped stitch over (skpo) This
method involves slipping a stitch and then passing the next one over it, rather like casting off. This decrease slants to the left on a knit row.

  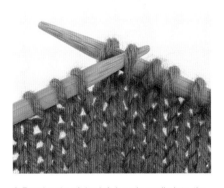

1 Knit to the position of the decrease. Put the right-hand needle into the next stitch, as if you were going to knit it, but slip it from the left-hand to the right-hand needle without knitting it.

2 Knit the next stitch on the left-hand needle in the usual way.

3 Put the tip of the left-hand needle into the slipped stitch and lift it over the knitted stitch, then drop it off both needles.

You have made two stitches into one and so decreased by one stitch.

short-row shaping

This is a common method of turning the heel on a sock. Each row will tell you to knit a number of stitches, then 'wrap next st, turn'. Follow these wrapping techniques to wrap the next stitch in the row, then turn the knitting by swapping the needles in your hands.

on a knit row Knit the number of stitches stated then wrap the next stitch as follows.

1 Slip the next stitch on the left-hand needle purlwise onto the right-hand needle (see page 122).

2 Bring the yarn forward between the tips of the needles.

3 Now slip the stitch back onto the left-hand needle, then take the yarn to the back again, thus wrapping it around the slipped stitch. Here, the yarn is shown as a loop so that you can see what is happening, but you must pull it taut. Now you are ready to turn the work and purl the next row.

on a purl row Purl the number of stitches stated then wrap the next stitch as follows.

1 Slip the next stitch on the left-hand needle purlwise onto the right-hand needle (see page 122).

2 Take the yarn back between the tips of the needles.

3 Now slip the stitch back onto the left-hand needle, then bring the yarn to the front between the needles again, thus wrapping it around the slipped stitch. Now you are ready to turn the work and knit the next row.

picking up wraps on a knit row
Once the shaping rows are completed, you will knit across all the stitches in the row to start the foot section of the sock. When doing this it is essential to knit the wrap loops together with the slipped stitches they encircle to prevent holes forming. Follow the technique shown on each wrapped stitch as you get to it.

From the front and using the tip of the right-hand needle, pick up the wrap loop around the base of the slipped stitch. Slip this loop onto the tip of the left-hand needle and then knit the loop and stitch together as if they were one. The loop will not be visible on the right side of the work.

picking up wraps on a purl row
Working across the knitting in the opposite direction to a knit row, follow the technique shown on each wrapped stitch as you get to it.

From behind and using the tip of the right-hand needle, pick up the wrap loop around the base of the slipped stitch. Slip this loop onto the tip of the left-hand needle and then purl the loop and stitch together as if they were one. The loop will not be visible on the right side of the work.

cables

Cabling is one of those techniques that looks difficult, but is in fact easy. All you are doing is swapping the positions on the needle of groups of stitches. Shown here is cable four but you can cable two, four or six stitches just as easily. Cables are usually worked in stocking stitch with a background of reverse stocking stitch, as shown.

cable four back (C4B) A back cable twists
to the right on the right side of the work.

1 Purl to the position of the cable. Take the yarn between the tips of the needles to the back of the work.

2 Slip the next two stitches on the left-hand needle onto a cable needle.

3 With the cable needle at the back of the work, knit the next two stitches on the left-hand needle. Just ignore the cable needle while doing this.

4 Now knit the two stitches on the cable needle. Just slide them to the end of the needle and knit them in the usual way. Purl to the end of the row, or to the next cable.

cable four front (C4F) A front (or 'forward',
as it is also known) cable twists to the left on the right side of the work. Work it in a similar way to a front cable, but leave it at the front of the work instead of at the back while you knit the next two stitches on the left-hand needle.

Left: this swatch of C4B is worked over eight rows; that is to say, the cable is twisted on every eighth row of knitting.

crosses

Crossed stitches use the same principle as cables, but are subtler and so often used with other stitches to produce effects like lace. Here, the technique is shown on reverse stocking stitch: to work it on stocking stitch, knit the stitches instead of purling them.

cross three right (cr3R) The stitches
cross to the right on the right side of the work.

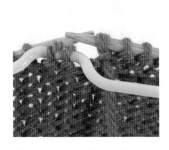 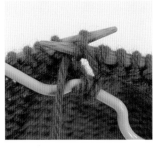 

cross three left (cr3L)

The stitches cross to the left on the right side of the work. Work this in a similar way to cr3R, but slip just one stitch onto the cable needle and leave it at the back of the work. Purl two stitches from the left-hand needle, then purl the stitch from the cable needle.

1 Purl to the position of the cross. Slip the next two stitches on the left-hand needle onto a cable needle and leave this at the front of the work.

2 Purl the next stitch on the left-hand needle.

3 Then purl the two stitches from the cable needle. Purl along to the next stitch instruction.

bobbles

Bobbles can be big and chunky or small and sweet and there are various different ways to produce them; shown here is the technique used in this book.

1 Knit to the position of the bobble. Knit into the front and back of the next stitch in the same way as for inc (see page 116), but do this twice so that you have made four stitches out of one.

2 Turn the work by swapping the needles in your hands. Purl the four stitches created in Step 1. Turn the work again and knit the four stitches.

3 Turn the work again. Work p2tog (see page 117) twice to reduce the four stitches to two.

4 Turn the work for the last time and work k2tog (see page 117) to reduce the two stitches to one and thus complete the bobble and return to the original stitch count on the row.

Above: when you have completed the knitting you can tweak and shape the bobbles a little with your fingers if necessary.

yarnover (yo)

These are the staple ingredient of lace knitting. A yarnover produces a small eyelet that when arranged with others in a pattern produces the lace effect. Eyelets worked in this way are also used to make buttonholes for small buttons.

1 On a knit row, knit to the position of the eyelet. Bring the yarn forward between the tips of the knitting needles: this is known as 'yarnover' (yo).

2 Take the yarn over the top of the right-hand needle and to the back, ready to knit the next two stitches on the left-hand needle together (k2tog). When you are purling back across the stitches, purl the yarnover as if it were a normal stitch.

through the back loop (tbl)

Knitting or purling a stitch through the back of the loop (rather than through the front as normal), twists the stitch. The effect is subtle and is used mainly as either an element in lace knitting, or in shaping: for example, 'k2togtbl' means knit two together (see page 117), but through the back loops.

To knit a stitch through the back loop, put the right-hand needle from right to left through the stitch, but putting it behind the left-hand needle. Take the yarn around the tip of the right-hand needle in the usual way and knit the stitch.

To purl a stitch through the back loop, put the right-hand needle from left to right through the back of the stitch: when you straighten the left-hand needle the stitch will be twisted around it, as shown. Take the yarn around the tip of the right-hand needle in the usual way and purl the stitch.

slipping stitches

Another technique often used in lace knitting, slipped stitches can be worked knitwise or purlwise. If the pattern does not specify which way to slip a stitch, slip it knitwise on a knit row and purlwise on a purl row.

pick up and knit

Use this technique to start knitting from a piece that has been cast off. It is another way of turning a sock heel. The knitting pattern will tell you where and how many stitches to pick up.

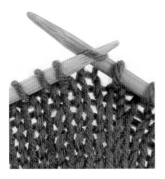

1 On a knit row, slip a stitch knitwise by putting the right-hand needle into the next stitch, as if to knit it, but slip it onto the needle without actually knitting it. Knit the next stitch in the usual way.

2 The principle is the same if you are slipping a stitch purlwise. Put the right-hand needle into the next stitch, as if to purl it, but slip it onto the needle without actually purling it. Knit the next stitch in the usual way.

1 Hold the yarn from which you are going to pick up the new stitches at the back of the finished piece. Put a knitting needle through the middle of the first stitch to be picked up from. At the back, loop the yarn over the tip of the needle.

2 Bring the needle back through the stitch, bringing the loop of yarn through with it. You have picked up one stitch.

swiss darning

Also known as duplicate stitch, this is a way of adding different-coloured stitches to a piece of knitting once it is finished. Always work Swiss darning using a yarn that is the same weight as the yarn the fabric is knitted in or it won't look very neat.

a vertical row Use this method to work vertical rows of coloured stitches.

a horizontal row Use this method to work horizontal rows of coloured stitches.

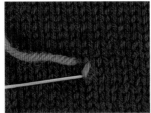

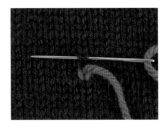

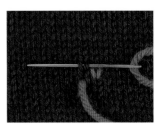

1 Thread a knitter's sewing needle with a long length of yarn. From the back, bring the needle up through the knitted fabric at the base of a stitch. *Take the needle under the two loops of the stitch above, as shown.

2 Gently pull the yarn through, then take the needle back down through the base of the stitch, where it came out.

3 Bring the yarn up through the knitted fabric at the base of the next stitch up. Repeat from * until the row is stitched.

From the back, bring the needle up through the knitted fabric at the base of a stitch. Take the needle under the two loops of the stitch above and back down where it came out, as before. Bring the needle up through the base of the next stitch to the left to work the horizontal row.

colour knitting

There are two main techniques for colour knitting, Fair Isle and intarsia. However, note that the intarsia technique does not work if you are knitting in the round as the yarn will end up on the wrong side of the motif each time. For both techniques it is important to twist the yarns around one another as shown to prevent holes appearing between the different-coloured yarns. Whether colours change in straight lines or on the diagonal will, of course, depend on the motif you are knitting. Shown here are the principles of making all the colour changes.

fair isle This method strands yarn across the back of the work and is used to knit continuous patterns and motifs in the round. When using this technique, do not pull the yarn tight across the back of the work or it will pucker up. However, stranding it too loosely will result in loops that catch on your toes. Practise the technique to get the balance right before starting a project.

1 On a knit row, knit to the first colour change. Bring the new colour yarn (purple) from under the original colour yarn (pink) and then around the needle to knit the stitch.

2 Knit the stitches in the new colour yarn. When you get to the next colour change, bring that yarn (pink) from under the new colour yarn (purple) and around the needle to knit the stitch.

3 if the interval between colour changes is more than three stitches, you will need to weave the yarn not in use into the back of a stitch to prevent long loops forming on the back. Bring the working yarn under the yarn not in use, then knit the next stitch in the working yarn. Here the purple yarn is being woven in to the back of a pink stitch.

4 On a purl row, purl to the first colour change. Bring the new colour yarn (purple) under the original colour (pink) and then around the needle to purl the stitch.

5 At the next colour change, bring the original yarn (here it is pink) over the new yarn (purple) and purl the stitches.

6 If the interval between colour changes is more than three stitches you must also weave in the yarn not in use on purl rows. Use the same procedure as for knit rows.

Above: where the yarn not in use is woven into the back of a stitch it may well show a little on the front, either as a slight pucker in the stitch or as a spot of colour between stitches. This is inherent in Fair Isle knitting.

intarsia This method uses a separate ball of yarn for each coloured area. To avoid tangling the yarns, wind long lengths onto bobbins and knit from these.

1 On a knit row, knit to the first colour change. Bring the new colour yarn (magenta) over the original colour yarn (blue) and then around the needle to knit the stitch.

2 Knit the stitches in the new colour yarn. When you get to the next colour change, bring that yarn (magenta) over the original colour yarn (blue) and around the needle to knit the stitch. To knit the next stitch on the row shown, bring the blue yarn over the magenta yarn: this is shown below on a purl row where it can be seen more easily.

3 On a purl row, purl to the first colour change. Bring the new colour yarn (magenta) under the original colour yarn (blue) and then around the needle to purl the stitch.

4 Purl the stitches in the new colour yarn. When you get to the next colour change, bring that yarn (magenta) under the original colour yarn (blue) and around the needle to knit the stitch.

5 To work the next colour change, bring the new colour (now blue) over the old colour (magenta) on both knit and purl rows.

Above: Weaving in ends neatly (see page 125) gives you the opportunity to tighten up any loose stitches at the beginning and end of an intarsia colour motif.

using a stitch holder

Some patterns tell you to place a certain number of stitches on a holder. You will work the remaining stitches on the knitting needles, then come back to the stitches on the holder and work those.

Simply slip the required number of stitches from the needle onto the holder. Make sure that the holder is securely closed, then ignore it until the pattern tells you otherwise. At that point, slip the stitches back onto the needle and work them as instructed.

joining in new yarn

When you reach the end of a ball of yarn you need to join in a new one to continue knitting. You also use this method to join in a different-coloured yarn in colour knitting (see pages 123–124).

If you are joining in new yarn because you have come to the end of a ball, join it in at the end of a row. You must have a length of yarn approximately four times the width of the knitting to knit one row.

Tie the new yarn in a loose single knot around the tail end of the old yarn. Slide the knot up to the work and pull it tight. Leave a 15cm tail on each yarn to weave in later.

weaving in ends

When you have finished your knitting, you need to weave in any ends from casting on, casting off and joining in new yarn.

Thread a knitter's sewing needle with the tail of yarn. Take the needle back and forth, not up and over, through the backs of several stitches. Go through approximately four stitches in one direction, then work back through the last two again. If you are weaving in ends from colour knitting, weave the tails into stitches of the same colour to stop them showing on the front.

sewing up

Many people rush this stage of making a knitting project, which is a mistake. Take your time and your seams will be smooth and neat, giving your knitting a professional finish.

Use the yarn you used to knit the project in to sew it up, though if the yarn is very fine or breaks easily, use a stronger one in the same fibre and colour.

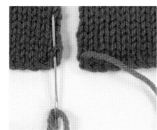

1 Thread a knitter's sewing needle with a long length of yarn. Here, a contrast colour has been used for clarity. Secure the yarn on the back of one of the pieces to be joined by taking it over a couple of stitches, a couple of times. Bring the needle to the front of the fabric, bringing it up between the first two stitches on the first row.

2 Right-side up, lay the other project piece to be joined next to the first piece. From the front, take the needle through the fabric between the first two stitches on the first row and up under the bars of two stitches. Pull the yarn through.

3 Take the needle back through where it came out on the first piece and up under the bars of two stitches. Take the needle back to the other piece, through where it came out and up under the bars of two stitches. Zigzag between the pieces, taking the needle under two stitch bars each time. Gently pull the yarn to close the seam as you work.

Above: worked neatly a mattress stitched seam blends in to the knitted fabric.

yarn information

Here is the fibre and meterage for all the yarns used in this book.

Anchor Arista Crochet yarn
80% viscose, 20% polyester
Approx 100m/25g ball

Debbie Bliss Cashmeriono DK
55% merino wool, 33%
microfibre, 12% cashmere
Approx 100m/50g ball

Debbie Bliss Pure Cashmere
100% cashmere
Approx 45m/25g ball

Debbie Bliss Rialto Aran
100% extra-fine merino wool
Approx 80m/50g ball

Garthenor 100% Organic Jacob
100% organic wool
Approx 68m/100g hank

Garthenor 100% Organic Shetland
100% organic Sheltland wool
Approx 113m/50g ball

Jaegar Matchmaker Merino 4-ply
100% merino wool
Approx 183m/50g ball

Jaegar Matchmaker Merino DK
100% merino wool
Approx 120m/50g ball

Jamieson's Shetland Heather Aran
(previously known as Jamieson's Soft Shetland)
100% wool
Approx 92m/50g ball

Patons Diploma Gold
55% wool, 25% acrylic, 20% nylon
Approx 120m/50g ball

Regia 4-ply
75% wool, 25% polyamide
Approx 210m/50g ball

Robin Double Knitting
100% acrylic
Approx 300m/100g ball

Rowan 4-ply Soft
100% merino wool
Approx 175m/50g ball

Rowan Cotton Glacé
100% cotton
Approx 115m/50g ball

Rowan Kid Classic
70% lambswool, 26% mohair, 4% nylon
Approx 140m/50g ball

Rowan Kidsilk Haze
70% kid mohair, 30% silk
Approx 210m/25g ball

Rowan Little Big Wool
67%wool, 33% nylon
Approx 60m/50g ball

Rowan Pure Wool DK
100% wool
Approx 125m/50g ball

Rowan RYC Baby Alpaca
100% baby alpaca wool
Approx 100m/50g ball

Rowan RYC Bamboo Soft
100% bamboo
Approx 102m/50g ball

Rowan RYC Cashsoft DK
57% extra-fine merino, 33% microfibre, 10% cashmere
Approx 130m/50g ball

Sirdar Country Style
45% acrylic, 40% nylon, 15% wool
Approx 318m/100g ball

substituting yarn

If you decide to use a yarn that is different to the one suggested, please follow these simple rules before buying.

Firstly, do use a yarn that is the suggested weight, even if you choose a different brand. If you use a DK-weight where the project asks for a chunky weight, you will run into problems.

Secondly, it is the number of metres of yarn in each ball, not the weight of the ball, that is important. Balls of different brands of yarn, even if they are the same weight, will not necessarily contain the same number of metres of yarn. So you cannot just buy the number of balls the pattern asks for in your substitute yarn: you need to do two sums, but they are simple ones.

Given left is the number of metres per ball for the yarns used in the projects. Multiply the appropriate number of metres by the number of balls needed to knit the project. This will give you the total number of metres of yarn you need.

Now check the ball band of your substitute yarn to see how many metres there are in a ball. Divide the total number of metres needed by the number in one ball of the substitute yarn and this will tell you how many balls of that yarn you need to buy.

Before you start knitting the project, you absolutely must knit a tension swatch in the substitute yarn to check that it will achieve the tension stated in the pattern.

resources

Lowie can be contacted at info@ilovelowie.com

UK

Arista crochet yarns
Patons yarns
Coats Crafts UK
PO Box 22
Lingfield House
Lingfield Point
McMullen Road
Darlington
County Durham DL1 1YQ
Tel: 01325 394237
www.coatscrafts.co.uk

Debbie Bliss yarns
Designer Yarns Ltd
Units 8-10 Newbridge Industrial Estate
Pitt Street
Keighley
West Yorkshire, BD21 4PQ
Tel: 01535 664222
Fax: 01535 664333
www.designeryarns.uk.com

Garthenor yarns
Garthenor Organic Pure Wool
Llanio Road
Tregaron
SY25 6UR
Tel: 0845 4082437
www.organicpurewool.co.uk

Jamieson's yarns
Jamieson's of Shetland
Tel: 01595 870285
www.jamiesonsshetland.co.uk

Jaeger yarns
Rowan yarns
Rowan Yarns and Jaeger Handknits
Green Lane Mill
Holmfirth
West Yorkshire HD9 2DX
Tel: 01484 681881
www.knitrowan.com

Robin yarns
Thomas B Ramsden & Co (Bradford) Ltd
Tel: 01943 872264
www.tbramsden.co.uk

Sirdar yarns
Sirdar Spinning Ltd
Flanshaw Lane
Wakefield
West Yorkshire
WF2 9ND
Tel: 01924 371501
www.sirdar.co.uk

USA

Arista crochet yarns
Coats & Clark
Consumer Services
P.O. Box 12229
Greenville
SC 29612-0229
Tel: (800) 648-1479
www.coatsandclark.com

Debbie Bliss yarns
Sirdar yarns
Knitting Fever Inc.
P.O. Box 502
Roosevelt
New York 11575
Tel: (516) 546 3600
www.knittingfever.com

Garthenor yarns
www.organicpurewool.co.uk

Jamieson's yarns
Simply Shetland
Tel: 877 743 8526
www.simplyshetland.net

Jaeger yarns
Regia yarns
Rowan yarns
Westminster Fibers Inc.

4 Townsend West
Suite 8
Nashua NH 03063
Tel: 603 886 5041
www.westminsterfibers.com

Patons yarns
Patons
320 Livingstone Avenue South
Listowel ON
Canada
N4W 3H3
tel: 1 888 368 8401
www.patonsyarn.com

CANADA
Debbie Bliss yarns
Regia yarns
Rowan yarns
Sirdar yarns
Diamond Yarns Ltd
155 Martin Ross Avenue
Unit 3
Toronto
Ontario M3J 2L9
Tel: 001 416 736 6111
www.diamondyarn.com

Garthenor yarns
www.organicpurewool.co.uk

Jamieson's yarns
Simply Shetland
Tel: 877 743 8526
www.simplyshetland.net

Patons yarns
Patons
320 Livingstone Avenue South
Listowel ON
Canada
N4W 3H3
tel: 1 888 368 8401
www.patonsyarn.com

acknowledgements

I couldn't have made this book by myself so I'd like to thank these great people for helping make it happen.
Thank you to Cindy Richards for being a fabulous publisher and having the insight to know that this was the right book to do; my editor, Kate Haxell, who is an impressive source of information and inspiration; my fabulous assistants, Katie and Naomi, and my interns, Bekki and Tosha, for helping with all the little extras that needed doing; Sally Powell, my extremely helpful Cico contact, and Liz Sephton for her lovely book design; Dygo Uetsuji and Becky Maynes for photography, Sue Whiting and Penny Hill for all the great patterns. Thank you also to my favourite friend Sally Jackson for bringing the lovely child models, Savannah and Isla, all the way from the countryside especially for this book and also to our gorgeous male model, Jonathon. Thank you also to all these knitters who turned my design dreams into reality: Pat, Mary, Dorothy, Frances, Margaret, Kate and Ann.

index